MACHINE LEARNING WITH SCRATCH 3.0

A PROJECT BASED APPROACH FOR KIDS

MEHAK JAIN

Made with ♥ on the Notion Press Platform
www.notionpress.com

This book is dedicated to my kids Virat and Naira...

Contents

Preface

As we move further into the 21st century, the world around us is becoming increasingly intelligent—smart homes, voice assistants, facial recognition, and even self-driving cars are no longer science fiction. At the heart of all these innovations lies Machine Learning—a fascinating field where computers learn from data and make decisions, just like humans do.

With this book, Machine Learning with Scratch, I wanted to open the doors of this exciting world to our youngest and most curious minds—kids and early learners. As an AI educator and a mother, I believe that if children can grasp the logic behind games and puzzles, they can certainly understand the foundations of Machine Learning—if taught the right way.

This book is a fun, engaging, and hands-on introduction to Machine Learning, specifically tailored for young learners aged 12 and above. It doesn't require any prior coding experience. By using Scratch 3.0, a visual programming language that's already popular among kids, and integrating it with the Machine Learning for Kids platform, we make learning both approachable and playful.

You'll find step-by-step instructions to build exciting projects—from cracking CAPTCHAs and sorting images, to creating smart homes and number recognition games. Along the way, readers will understand how different types of data help train machine learning models, and how those models can be used to solve real-world problems in creative ways.

More than just teaching a technical skill, this book aims to spark curiosity, problem-solving, and innovation. It invites kids to explore, experiment, and most importantly, to have fun while learning.

I hope that by the time they finish this book, young readers will not only understand what Machine Learning is, but also feel confident enough to build their own intelligent systems, and imagine new possibilities for the future.

Let the journey begin—one block, one idea, and one smart project at a time!

Warm wishes,

Mehak Jain

Acknowledgements

I would like to express my heartfelt gratitude to all the curious young minds who inspire me every day. Special thanks to educators, parents, and technology enthusiasts who believe in early learning and continue to support innovative teaching methods.
A huge shoutout to the team behind "Machine Learning for Kids" and Scratch 3.0 for making powerful tools accessible to children around the world.
Lastly, thank you to my family for being my biggest supporters and to the readers—this book is for you!

CHAPTER ONE

INTRODUCTION

What is Machine Learning?

Machine Learning is a branch of artificial intelligence where computers learn from data and experience to make predictions or decisions without being explicitly programmed.

It involves training models on large amounts of data to recognize patterns, and then using those models to make predictions on new, unseen data.

Essentially, it's teaching a computer to "learn" and improve its performance on tasks based on the data it processes, much like humans learn from experience.

In this book we will be using the below mentioned educational platform to train our machine learning models:

Machine Learning for Kids: https://machinelearningforkids.co.in/

This is an educational platform that introduces children to machine learning through hands-on-projects.

It offers resources and tools to teach kids how to train and test machine learning models using simple datasets. This site combines playful and practical learning, guiding children in creating their own AI-powered applications while enhancing their understanding of AI concepts.

The basic concepts of machine learning include:

1. **Data:** The foundation for any machine learning model, consisting of examples or observations.
2. **Algorithms**: Step-by-step procedures that the model follows to learn patterns from data.
3. **Training:** The process of feeding data to the algorithm to create a model.
4. **Features:** The characteristics or attributes used to make predictions.
5. **Labels:** The outcomes or results that model is trying to predict.
6. **Model:** The learned function or representation from the training process.
7. **Prediction:** The model's attempt to make decisions based on new data.
8. **Evaluation:** Testing the model's accuracy on unseen data.

Types of Training Data for a machine learning model

To train a machine learning model in AI, the type of data required depends on the problem you are trying to solve. Here's an overview of the types of data used for different purposes:

1. Labeled Data (for Supervised Learning)

- **Definition:** Labeled data is data that has both the input (features) and the correct output (label) provided. This type of data is used for supervised learning where the goal is to learn a mapping from inputs to outputs.
- **Example:** In an image classification problem, the images of cats and dogs (input) are labeled as "cat" or "dog" (output).
- **Usage:** Ideal for tasks like image classification, sentiment analysis, speech recognition, etc.

2. Unlabeled Data (for Unsupervised Learning)

- **Definition:** Unlabeled data has no output labels provided. The model needs to learn the underlying structure or patterns in the data.
- **Example:** In a clustering task, customer data (without knowing their groups) can be used to group similar customers based on their characteristics.
- **Usage:** Best for tasks like clustering, anomaly detection, and association rule mining.

3. Sequential Data (for Time-Series or Sequential Tasks)

- **Definition:** This type of data captures information over time or a sequence of steps.
- **Example:** Stock prices over time, temperature data, or language data where the order of the words matters (e.g., sentences).
- **Usage:** Used for models like recurrent neural networks (RNNs) in applications such as time-series forecasting or natural language processing (NLP).

4. Categorical Data

- **Definition:** Data that represents categories or discrete values.
- **Example:** Colors (red, blue, green), animal species (dog, cat), or binary values (yes/no).
- **Usage:** Useful in classification tasks where data needs to be assigned to different categories.

5. Numerical Data

- **Definition:** Data represented in numbers, either discrete or continuous.
- **Example:** Age, temperature or the number of items sold.
- **Usage:** Used in both regression tasks (predicting a numerical outcome) and for features in many other types of models.

6. Text Data

- **Definition:** Data in the form of written language.
- **Example:** Product reviews, social media posts or news articles.
- **Usage:** Used in NLP tasks such as sentiment analysis, text generation, or translation.

7. Image Data

- **Definition:** Visual data, often represented as pixels or image files.
- **Example:** Photographs, medical scans or handwritten digits.
- **Usage:** Used in tasks like image classification, object detection, and facial recognition.

8. Audio Data

- **Definition:** Sound data, typically in the form of waveforms.
- **Example:** Music recordings, speech or environmental sounds.
- **Usage:** Used in tasks like speech recognition, music classification or audio event detection.

9. Video Data

- **Definition:** A series of images (frames) that represent motion over time.

- **Example:** Video clips, surveillance footage.
- **Usage:** Used in applications like action recognition or video segmentation.

10. **Structured vs. Unstructured Data**

- **Structured Data:** Data that is organized and formatted, typically in tables (e.g., databases). It is easier to process and analyze. Example: Spreadsheets, SQL databases.
- **Unstructured Data:** Data that doesn't have a predefined format, making it more challenging to analyze. Example: Text documents, images, audio files.

Data Quality Considerations

Regardless of the type of data, the quality of data is crucial for the success of a machine learning model. Factors like accuracy, completeness, consistency, timeliness and relevance of the data play an important role in training effective models.

What is Scratch 3.0?

Scratch 3.0 is the version of Scratch, a free programming language and online community where kids can create their own interactive stories, animations and games.

It provides a block-based coding environment designed to make programming accessible to children and beginners.

Scratch 3.0 introduces enhanced features, including compatibility with mobile devices , new extensions for physical computing (like LEGO robots etc.), and a wide range of creative tools. It's widely used in schools to introduce coding concepts to young learners.

The basics of Scratch 3.0 involve using blocks to create programs by snapping them together.

Key elements include:

1. **Sprites:** Characters or objects you can control with code.
2. **Costumes:** Different appearances for sprites. You can switch costumes to create animation effects.
3. **Backdrop:** The background of the stage, which can be changed to set the scene.
4. **Stages:** The area where the action happens.
5. **Scripts:** Instructions created by stacking code blocks that control how sprites behave.
6. **Code Blocks:** Drag-and-drop blocks that represent commands, organized into categories (motion, looks, sound, events, etc.).

- Motion: Move, rotate or change the position of sprites.
- Looks: Change sprite appearance, say something or switch backdrops.
- Sound: Play sounds or music.
- Events: Trigger scripts (e.g. "when green flag clicked")
- Control: Loops, wait, if-else conditions etc.
- Sensing: Detect touch, mouse position or ask questions.
- Operators: Perform math or logic operations.
- Variables: Containers to store data, such as scores or timers, which can change during the program.
- My blocks: Custom blocks created by the user.

7. **Broadcast:** A way to send messages between different scripts, allowing sprites to interact.
8. **Loop:** Blocks that repeat actions such as "forever" or "repeat".

For the full course on Scratch 3.0 you can refer this video: https://www.youtube.com/watch?v=QFfCdY_sUp8

IMAGE RECOGNITION

CHAPTER TWO

PROJECT 1: COMPUTER CRACKS THE CAPTCHA

What is CAPTCHA?

CAPTCHA stands for Completely Automated Public Turing test to tell Computers and Humans Apart.

It's a type of challenge-response test used on websites to ensure that a user is human and not a computer program or bot.

Typically, it involves tasks like identifying distorted letters, selecting certain images (like identifying traffic lights or buses), or clicking a checkbox labeled "I'm not a robot". These tests are designed to be easy for humans but difficult for automated bots, helping to prevent spam, fraud, and other malicious activities online.

Can computers crack CAPTCHA?

Yes, computers are getting smarter and some can crack Captcha, but it's still not easy!

Overtime, clever programs called "bots" have been developed to try and solve Captchas. That's why CAPTCHA tests keep changing and getting harder to fool.

Objective: To train the computer to solve CAPTCHA.

Topics: Image recognition, supervised learning

Points to be noted:

- Only .jpg and .png images can be used otherwise an error message will be displayed.
- The more examples you give the machine learning model while training, the more efficient it will become. Below mentioned is the flowchart of this project

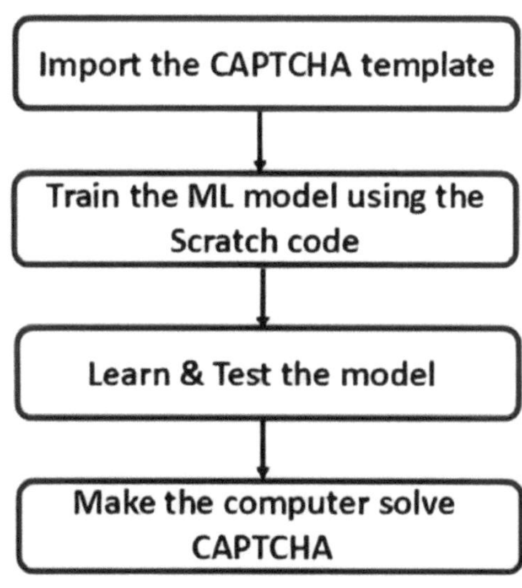

STEP BY STEP EXPLAINATION OF THE PROJECT
1. Click the below mentioned link and login.
MACHINE LEARNING FOR KIDS: https://machinelearningforkids.co.uk/
2. Go to your projects.
3. Click on "Copy template"

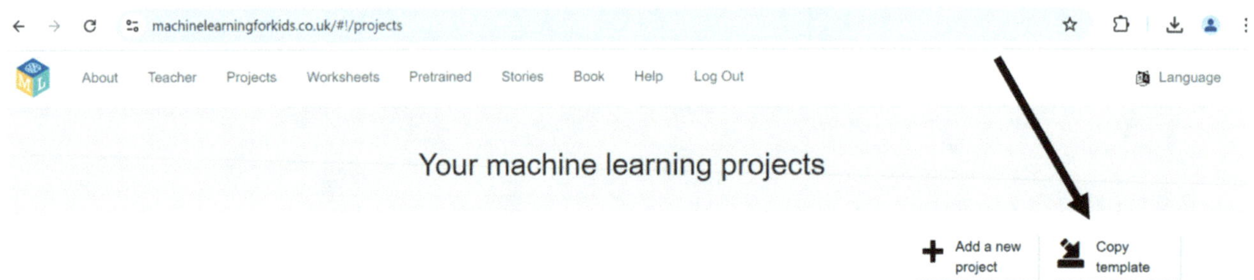

4. Import the project Captcha.

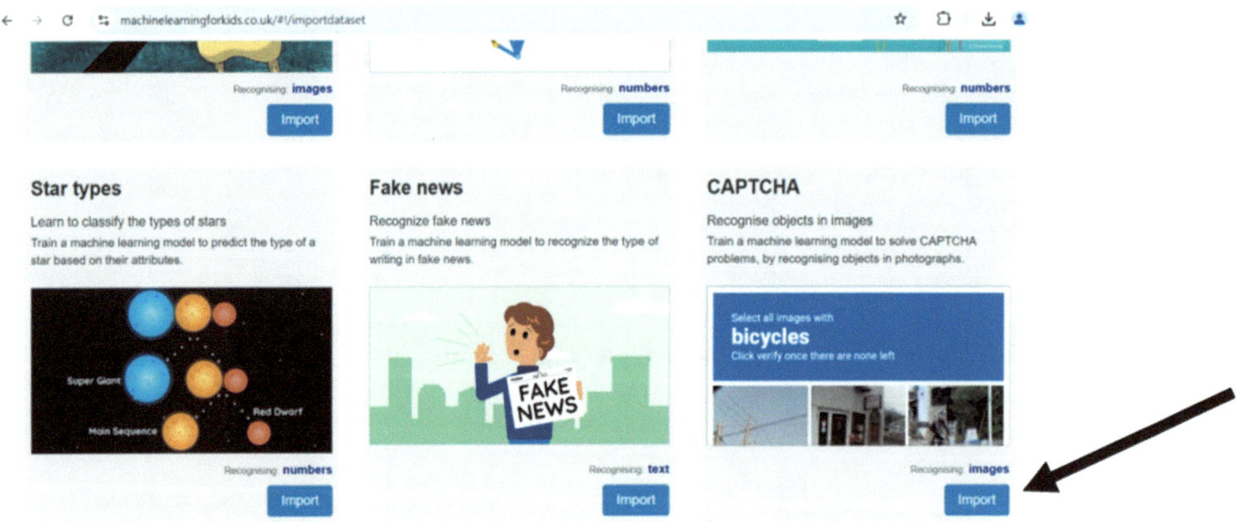

The project is imported.

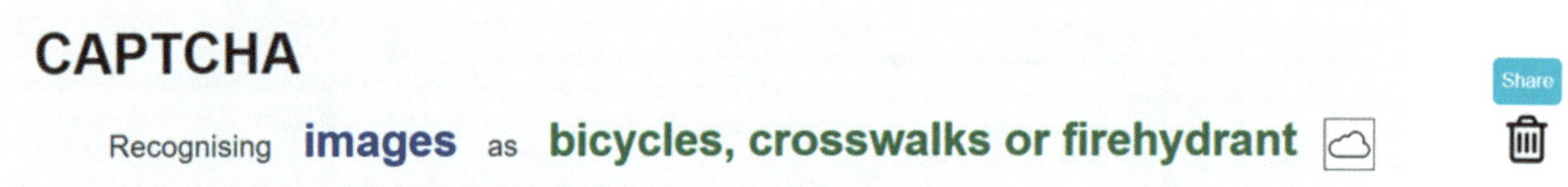

Stage 1: Training the Machine Learning model.
Now we'll be using the Scratch programming language to train the Machine Learning model.

5. Click on "Make".

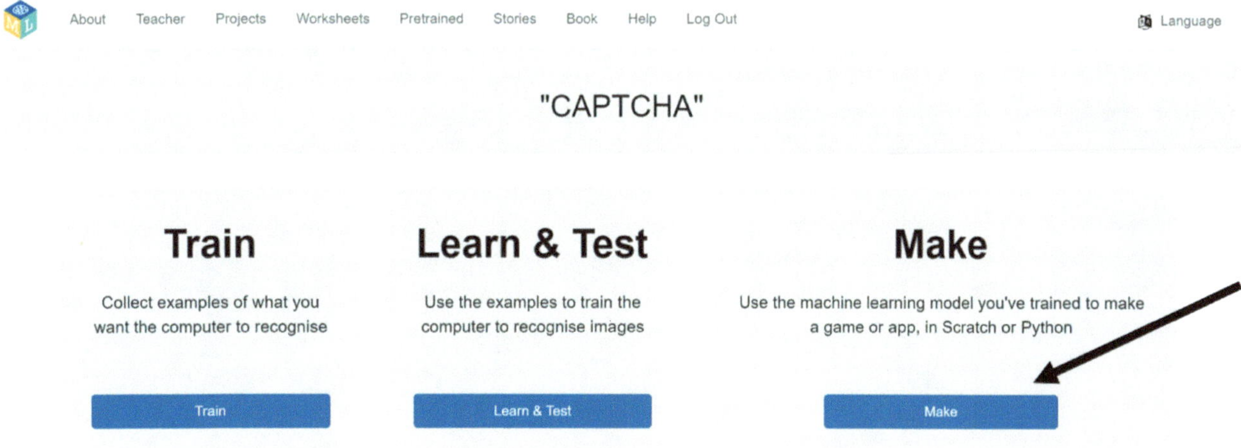

6. Click on "Scratch 3".

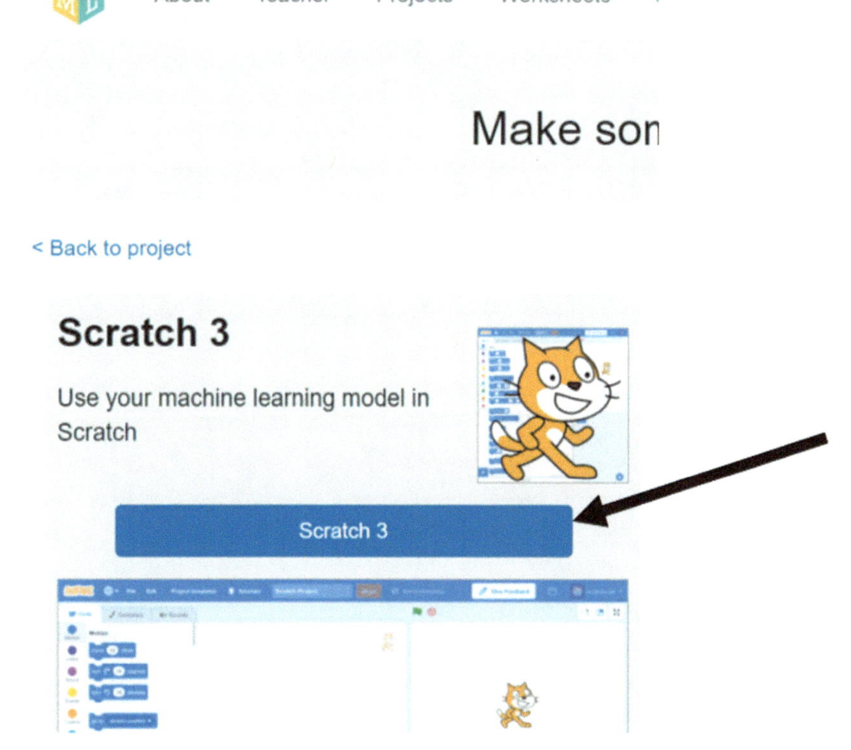

7. Click on "Project templates".

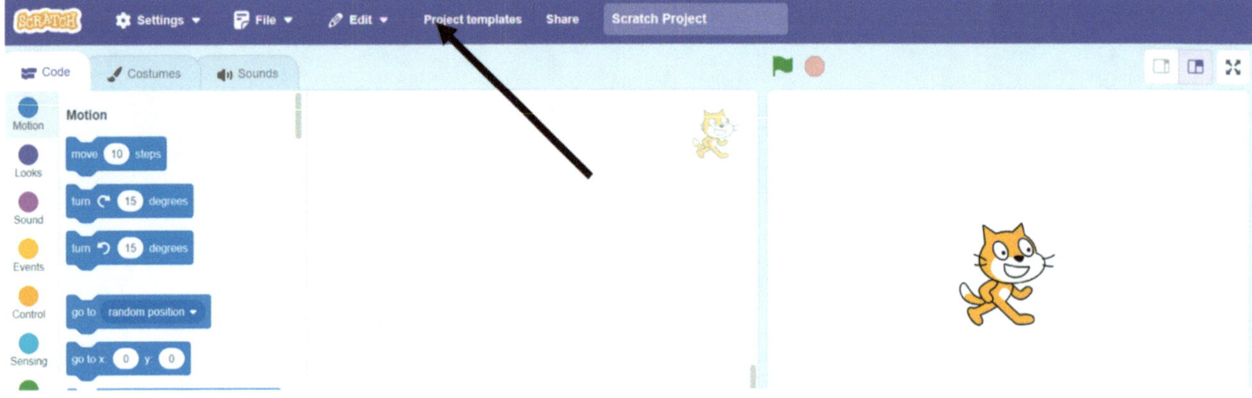

8. Click on "Captcha"

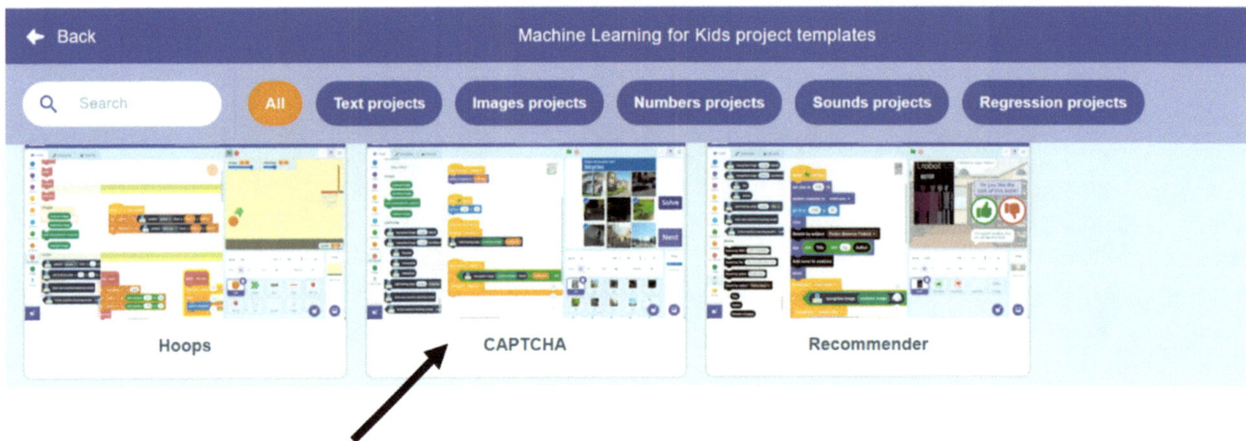

What do you observe in the Captcha Project template:

- There are total 20 sprites.
- 9 sprites compose the square grid of the captcha. Each sprite has 135 costumes each.

  This makes the project template very heavy.

- Other 9 sprites are the selected versions of the above-mentioned sprites.
- Sprite "Next" is used to display the next captcha.
- Sprite "Predict" is used to make the computer solve the Captcha using the trained Machine Learning model.
- The project template has 3 backdrops
- bicycles
- crosswalks
- fire hydrant

9. Click on the sprite "00" and update the code for the event "when this sprite clicked".

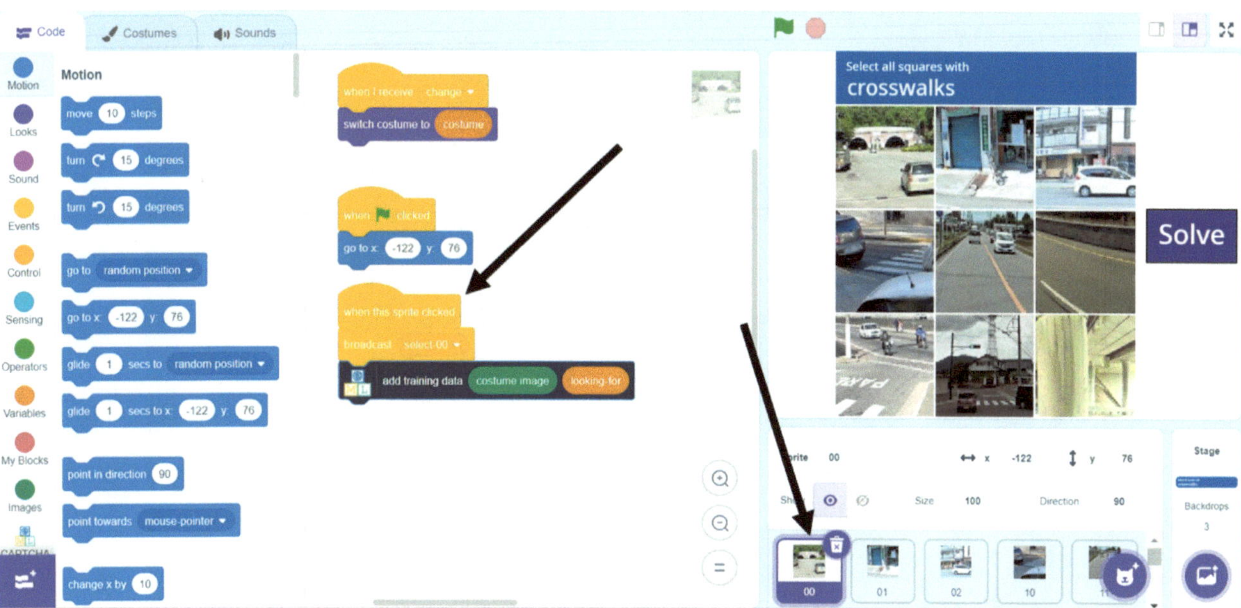

This is the code to be updated:

Now, also update the code for sprites 02,10,11,12,20,21,22 in a similar manner.

Note: The above updates will now be used to train the Machine Learning Model. This is an example of Supervised Learning.

Now, click on the Full Screen icon and then click on the Green flag.

Select the appropriate squares in the Captcha and then click "Next".

Repeat this at least 10 times so that the Machine Learning model is well trained and works efficiently.

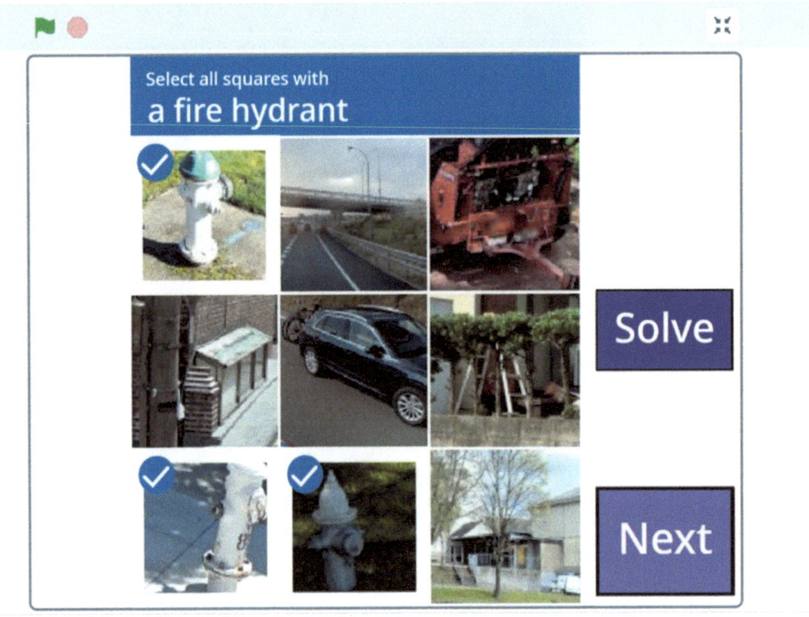

10. Now in the training tool tab, review the training data. Click on "Back to project" and then click on "Train".

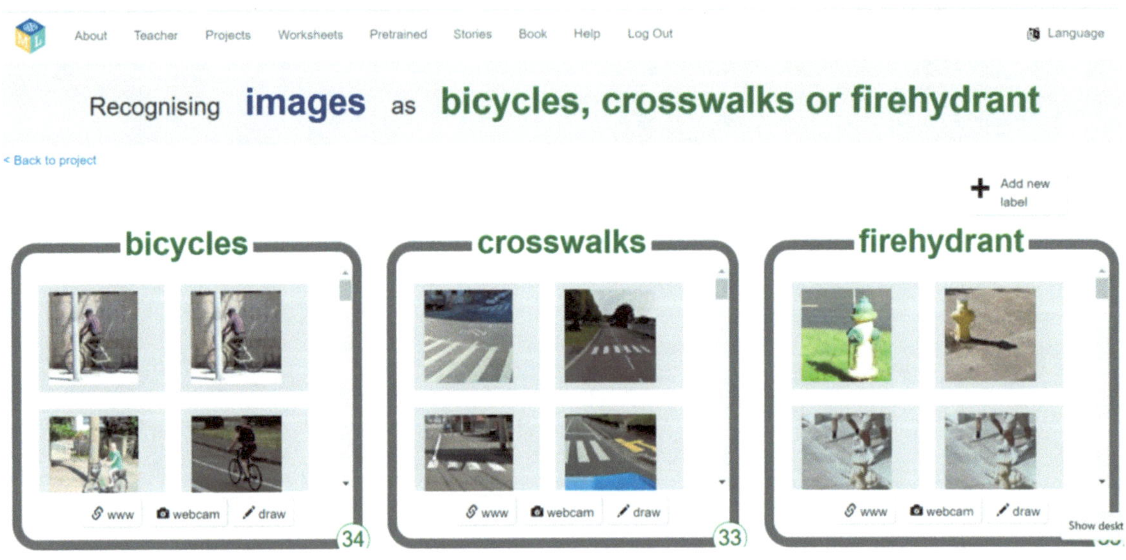

This is the data that we have collected using Scratch programming.

11. Click on "Back to project" and then click on "Learn & Test".

12. Click on "Train new machine learning model".

Here, the computer will learn from the patterns in the examples we have given it.

Stage 2: Making the computer solve the Captcha.

13. Click on the sprite "00" and update the code for the event "when I receive predict".

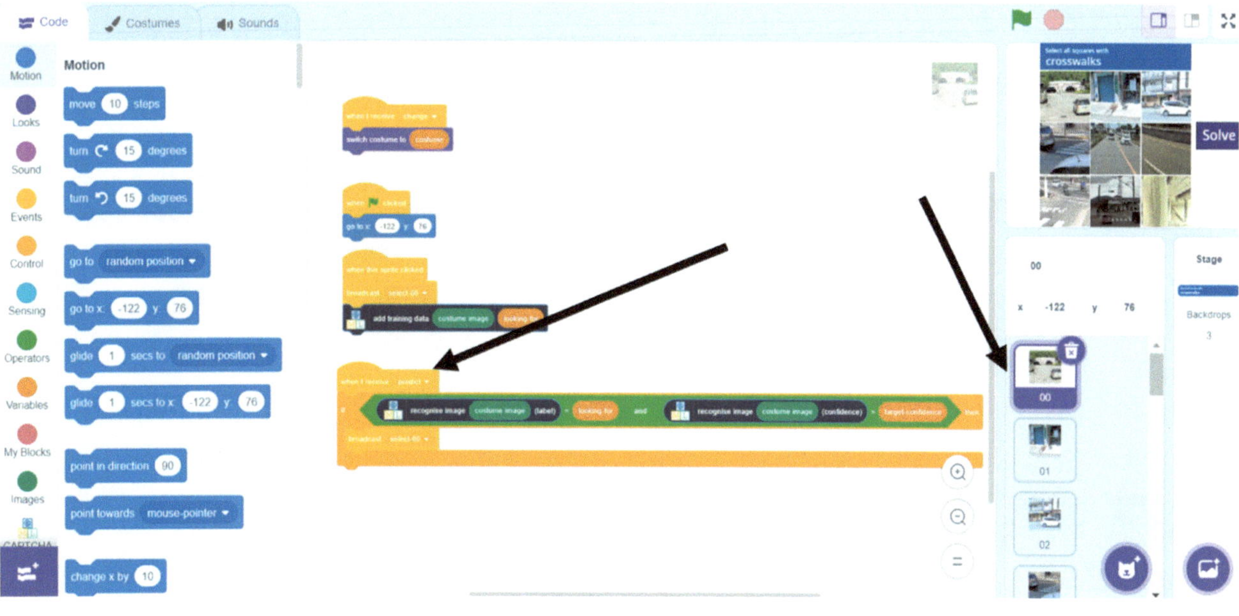

This is the code to be updated:

Now, also update the code for sprites 02,10,11,12,20,21,22 in a similar manner.

14. Click on the "predict" sprite and find the code for the event "when (green flag) clicked".

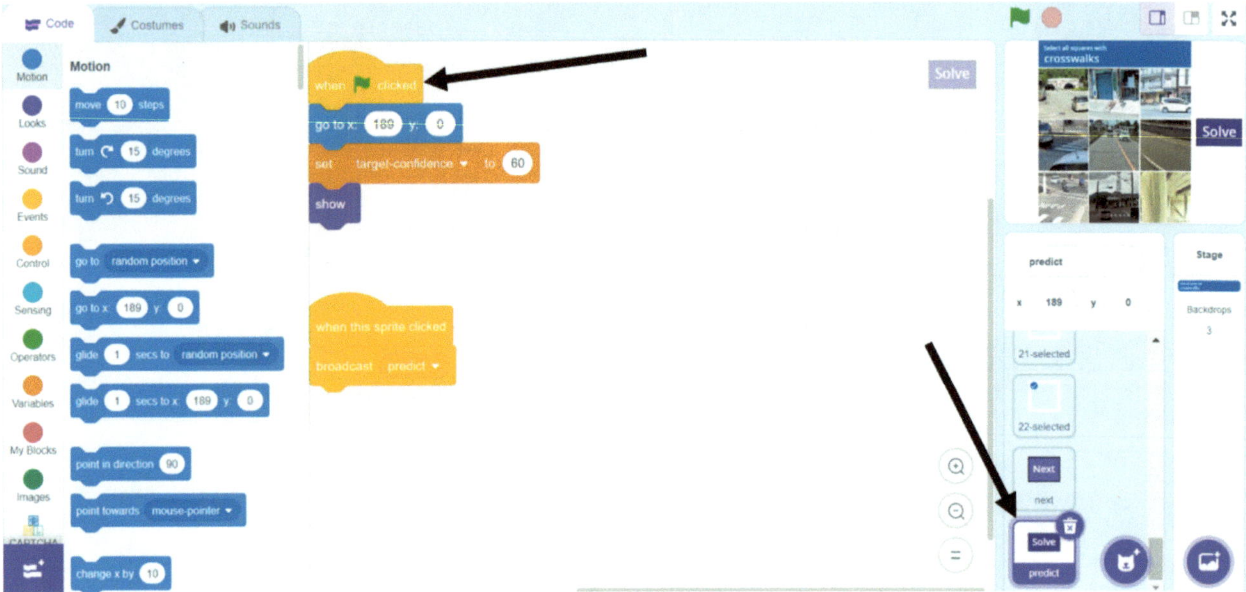

Replace "hide" to "show".

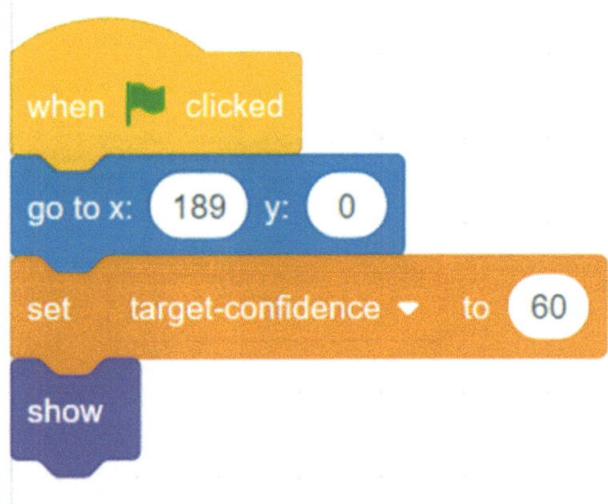

15. Click on "Full Screen" button & the Green flag & then click on "Solve".

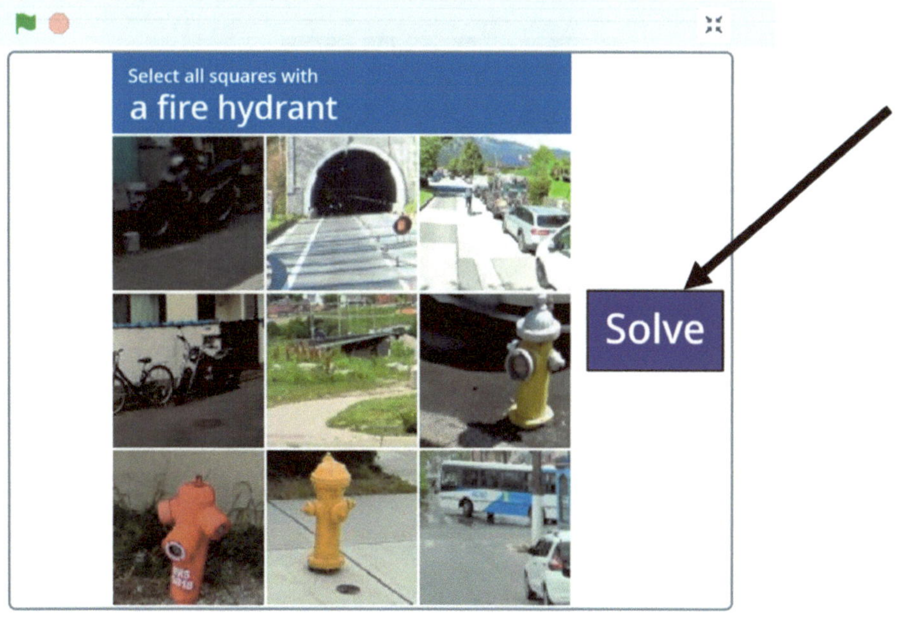

Now, you will see how the computer solves the Captcha using your trained Machine Learning model.

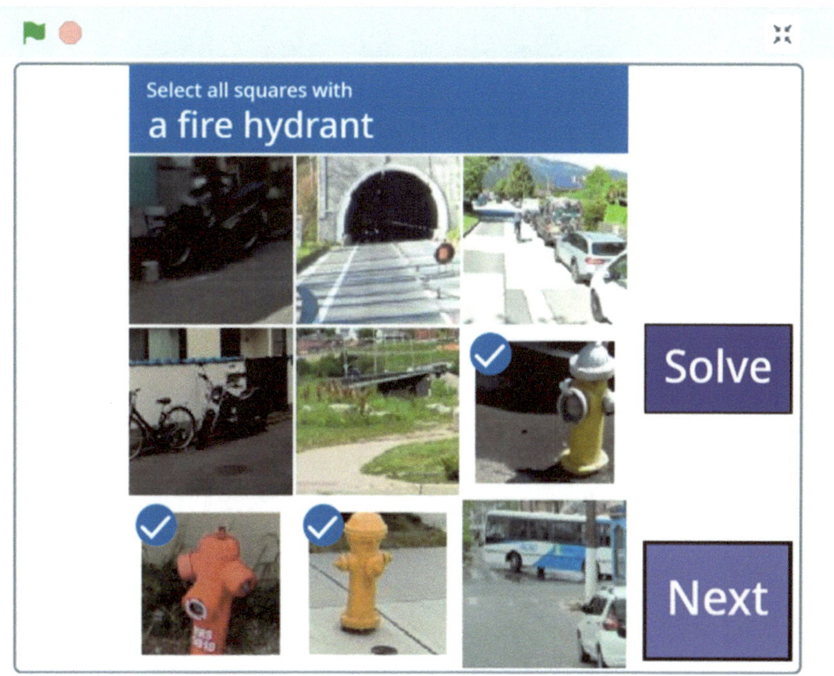

Scan the QR code to view the output of the project.

SCAN ME FOR THE OUTPUT VIDEO

CHAPTER THREE

PROJECT 2: AUTOMATIC IMAGE SORTER

OBJECTIVE: To train the computer to automatically sort images of frogs and ducks.
TOPICS: Image classification, supervised learning.
POINTS TO BE NOTED:

- Dragging and dropping doesn't work in Internet Explorer. You can use a different web browser instead such as Firefox or Chrome.
- You cannot drag and drop images between two different web browsers. For example, you cannot drag a picture from Chrome window to Machine Learning for kids in Firefox or vice versa.
- Only .jpg and .png images can be used otherwise an error message will be displayed.
- The more examples you give the machine learning model while training, the more efficient it will become.

STEP BY STEP EXPLAINATION OF THE PROJECT
Stage 1: Training the Machine Learning model to recognize images of frogs and ducks.
1. Click the below mentioned link and login.
MACHINE LEARNING FOR KIDS: https://machinelearningforkids.co.uk/

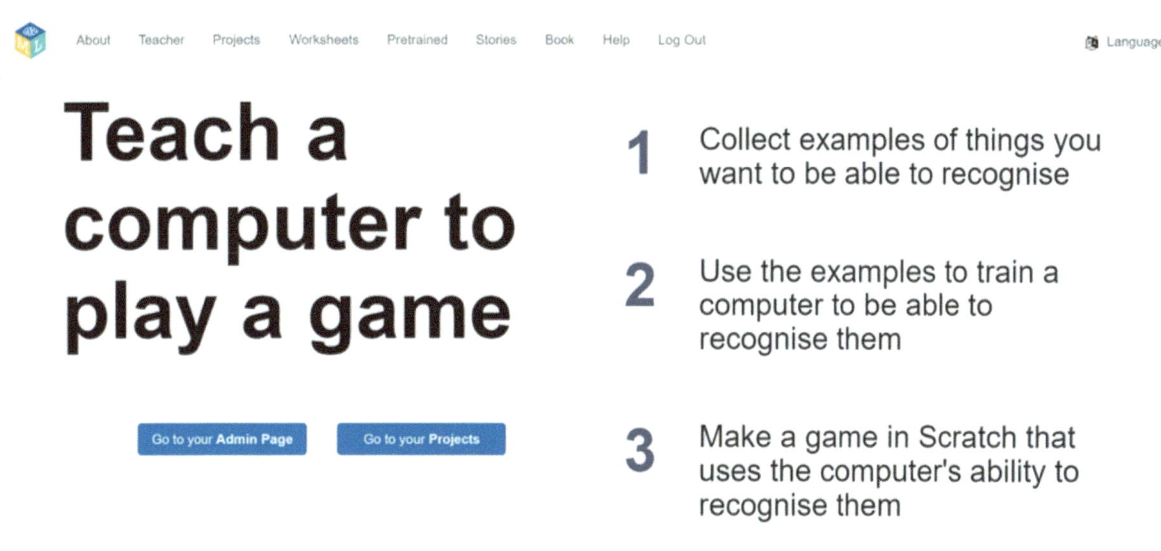

2. Click on "Go to your Projects".

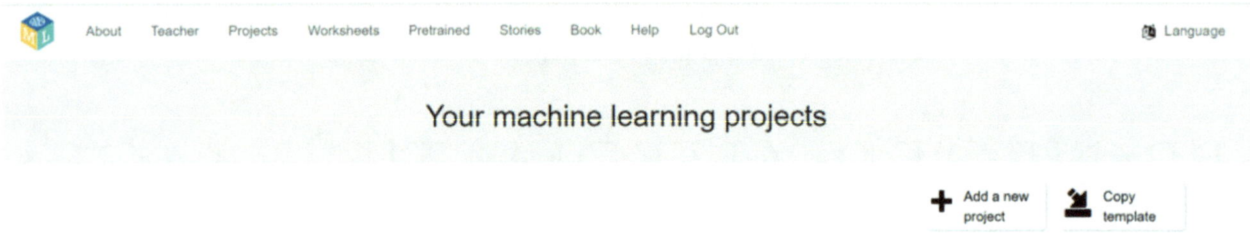

3. Click on "Add a new project". Enter the project name, project type and storage preference.

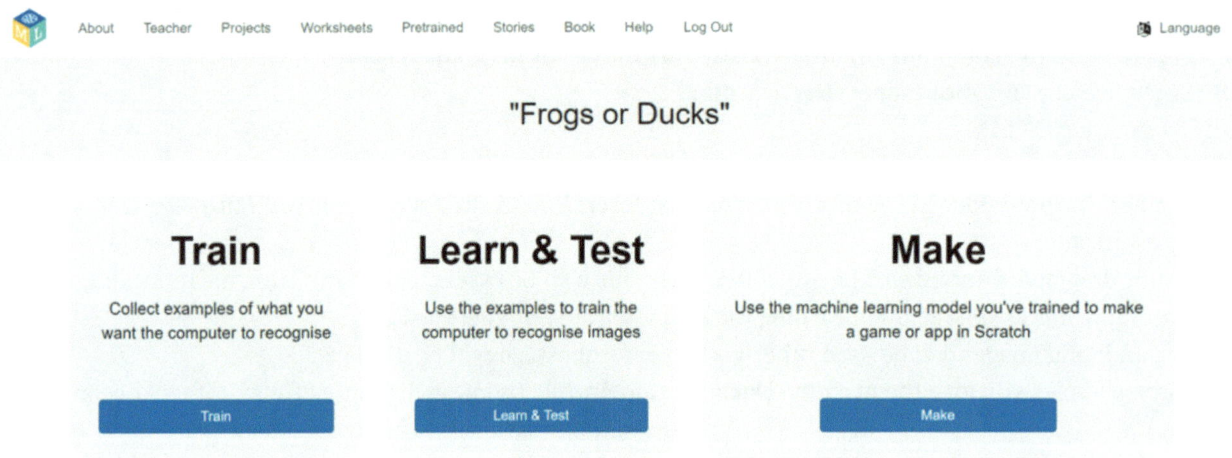

4. Click on "Train" to train the machine learning model to recognize frogs and ducks.

5. Click on "Add new label". Then add "Frog". Again, click on "Add new label". Then add "Duck"

6. Open another web browser window. Arrange the web browser windows such that they are side by side.

7. Drag pictures that are good examples of Frogs and Ducks. Make sure that the images are either .jpg or .png. otherwise, an error message will be displayed.

Collect at least 10 examples of Frog and Duck each to make the machine learning model work more effectively.

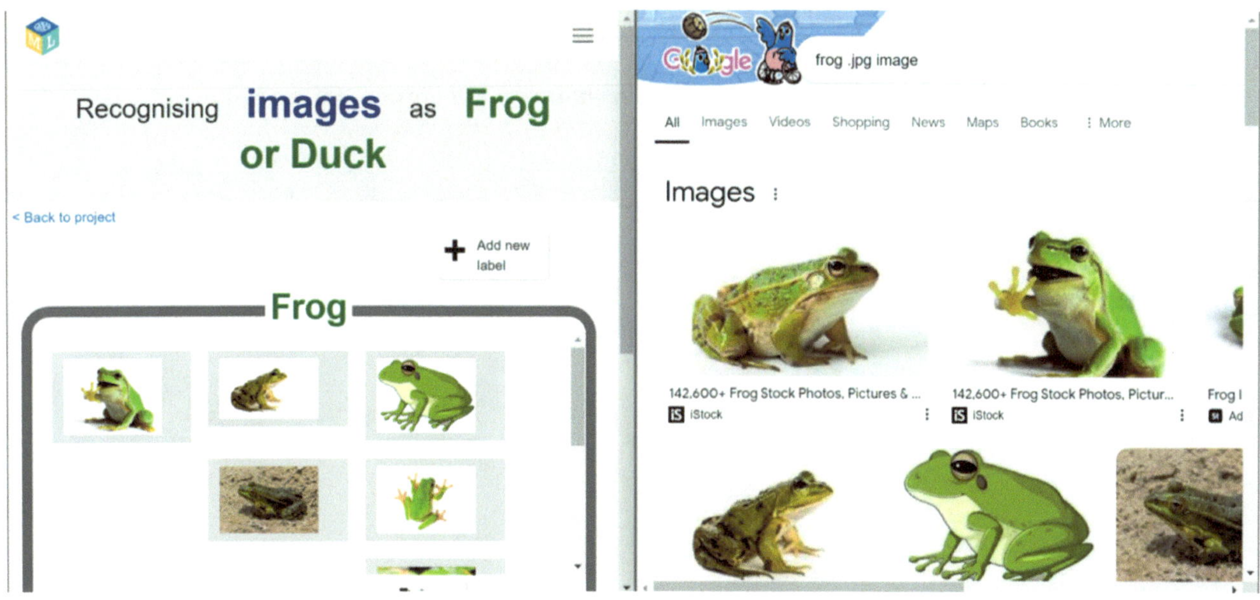

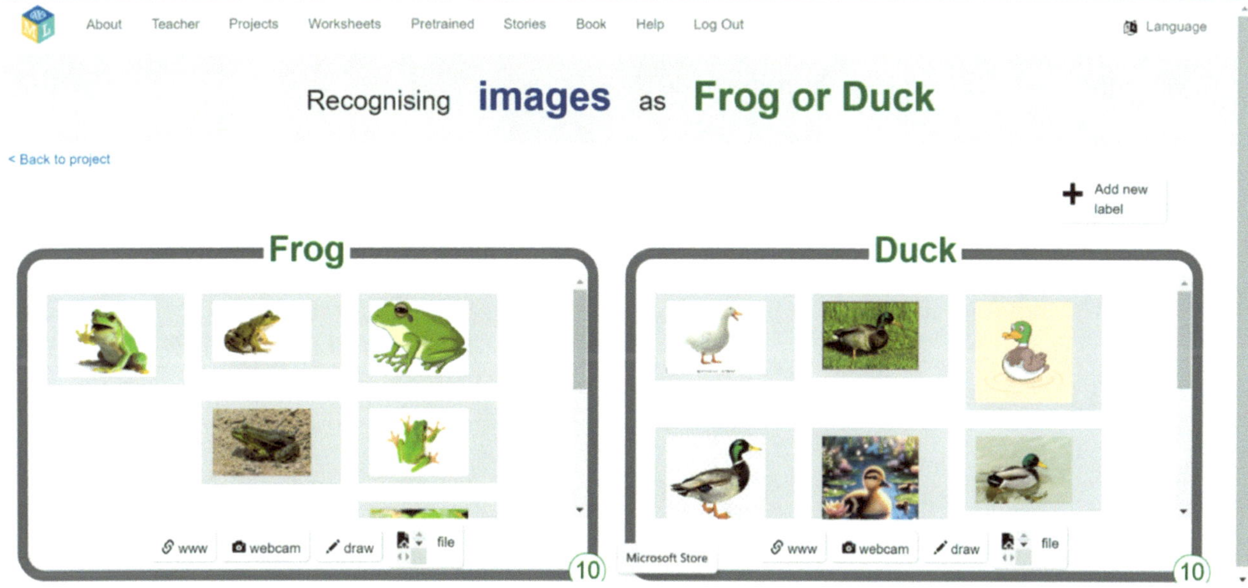

8. Click on "Back to project".

9. Then click on "Learn & Test". Here you can add an image and test how effective is the machine learning model after your training.

10. Click on "Back to project".

Stage 2: Coding in Scratch programming language to use the trained machine learning model.

11. Click on "Make".

Now we are going to use Scratch 3.0 to write the code to differentiate between frogs and ducks. Scratch 3.0 will use the machine learning model trained by us.

12. Click on "Scratch 3.0" then click on "Open in Scratch 3.0".

13. Create variables "y" and "item".

14. Click on the costumes tab.

15. Delete the existing costumes of the sprite and add atleast 10 new costumes of frogs and ducks to the existing sprite.

16. Choose a nice backdrop from the backdrop icon on the bottom right corner of the window.

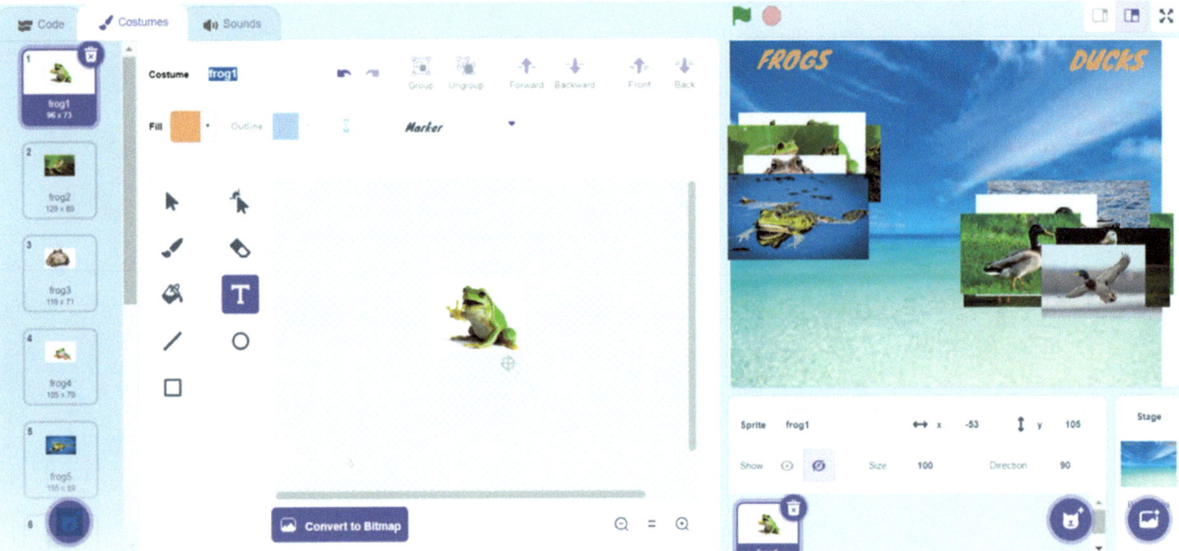

17. Click on the "Code" tab and copy the below code.

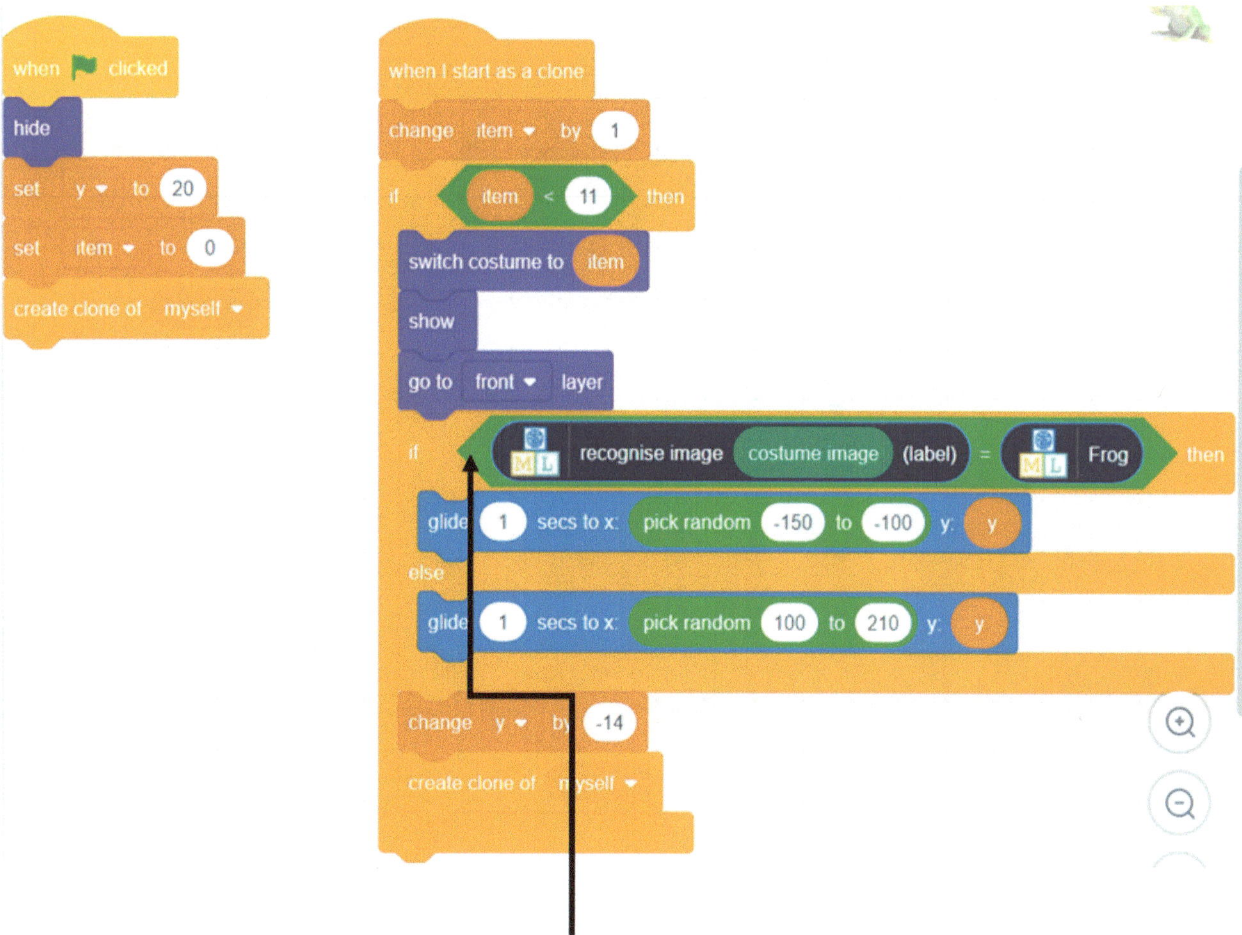

Integrating the trained machine learning model in Scratch.

Here, Scratch 3.0 is using the machine learning model trained by us to automatically sort frogs and ducks. More examples you give it during training, more efficient the machine learning model will become.
18. To run the project, click on the Green flag.
OUTPUT:

This is an **AUTOMATIC IMAGE SORTER**

Scan the QR code to view the output of the project.

SCAN ME FOR THE OUTPUT VIDEO

SOME REAL-LIFE APPLICATIONS OF IMAGE CLUSTERING

1. **Google Photos** (Photo organization): Google photos use image clustering to automatically group your photos based on people, places and things. It can recognize faces and create albums for different people or events.
2. **Handwriting Recognition:** Apps that convert handwritten notes into digital text like Google Keep or Microsoft OneNote, use image clustering to group and recognize similar letters or numbers. This makes it easier to turn messy handwriting into readable text.

3. **Medical Imaging**: In hospitals, software uses image clustering to help doctors by grouping similar medical images, like X-rays or MRIs. It can help identify patterns in these images, such as areas where there might be a broken bone or a tumor, making it easier for doctors to diagnose patients.
4. **Object detection in Autonomous vehicles**: Self-driving cars use image clustering to identify objects around them, such as other cars, pedestrians or traffic signs. By grouping these objects into clusters, the car can navigate safely through traffic.

CHAPTER FOUR

PROJECT 3: ROCK, PAPER AND SCISSORS

OBJECTIVE: Make the game Rock, Paper and Scissor.

In this project we will train the computer to recognize images of rock, paper and scissor in the player's captured photo. The computer generates a random move and the result is declared based on the player's captured move and computer's move.

TOPICS: Image classification, Reinforcement learning.

POINTS TO BE NOTED:

- Only .jpg and .png images can be used otherwise an error message will be displayed.
- The more examples you give the machine learning model while training, the more efficient it will become.

GENERAL RULES OF THE GAME:

The game Rock, Paper, Scissor is simple and fun! Here are the basic rules:

1. Players: Typically, it's played between 2 people. (Here it will be played between the computer and you.)
2. Choices: Each player simultaneously forms one of the three shapes with their hands:

- Rock (a closed fist)
- Paper (an open hand)
- Scissor (a fist with the index and the middle fingers extended, forming a V)

1. Gameplay: Players count to three together (or say "Rock, Paper, Scissor") and they reveal their chosen shape.
2. Winning conditions:

- Rock crushes Scissor (Rock wins)
- Scissor cuts Paper (Scissor wins)
- Paper covers Rock (Paper wins)

1. Ties: If both the players choose the same shape, it's a tie and they play again.

STEP BY STEP EXPLAINATION OF THE PROJECT
Stage 1: Training the Machine Learning model to differentiate between Rock, Paper and Scissor images.

1. Login to https://machinelearningforkids.co.uk/
2. Click on "Go to your Projects".
3. Click "Add a new project".

4. Enter the project name, project type and storage preference.
5. Click on "Train" to train the machine learning model .
6. Click on "Add new label". Then add "Rock", "Paper", "Scissor".
7. Click on "Webcam" and capture images of your hand making rock, paper and scissor.

Capture at least 10 examples of Rock, paper and scissor each to make the machine learning model work more effectively.

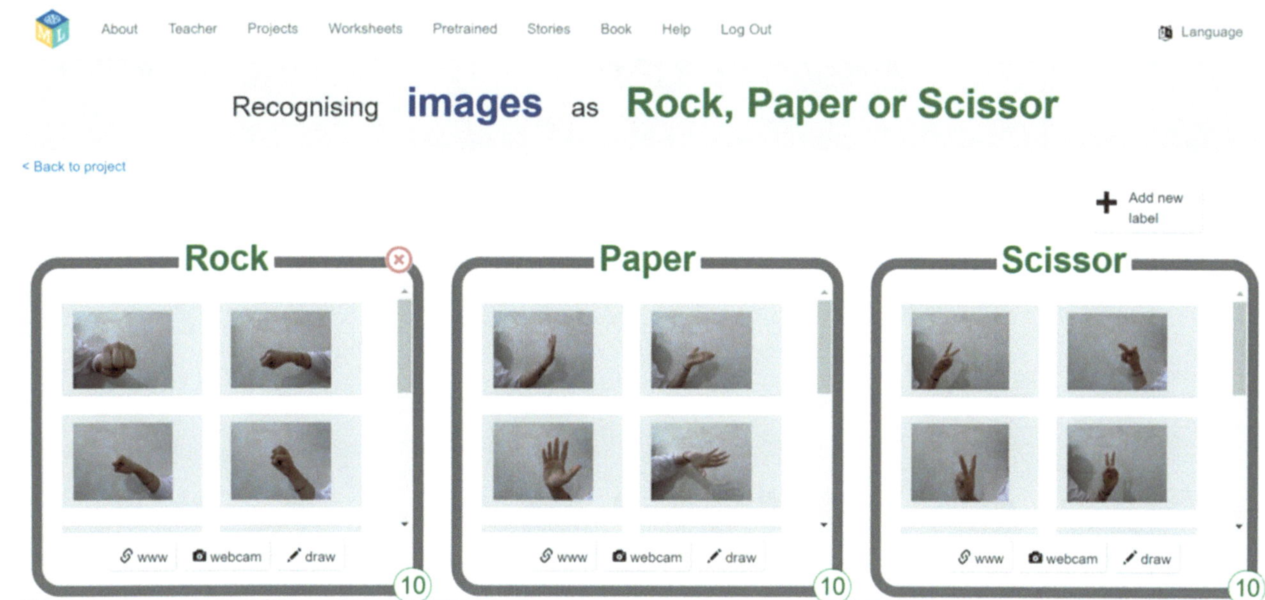

8. Click on "Back to project".

9. Then click on "Learn & Test".

Here you can use the "Test with webcam" option to capture an image and test how effective your machine learning model is.

10. Click "Back to project".

Stage 2: Coding in Scratch programming language to use the trained machine learning model.

11. Click on "Make".

Now we are going to use Scratch 3.0 to write the code to play a game of Rock, Paper and Scissor between the computer and the player.

12. Scratch 3.0 will use the machine learning model trained by us.

13. Click on "Scratch 3.0" then click on "Open in Scratch 3.0".

14. Delete the existing Sprite and create the following sprites.

Sprite 1: heading1

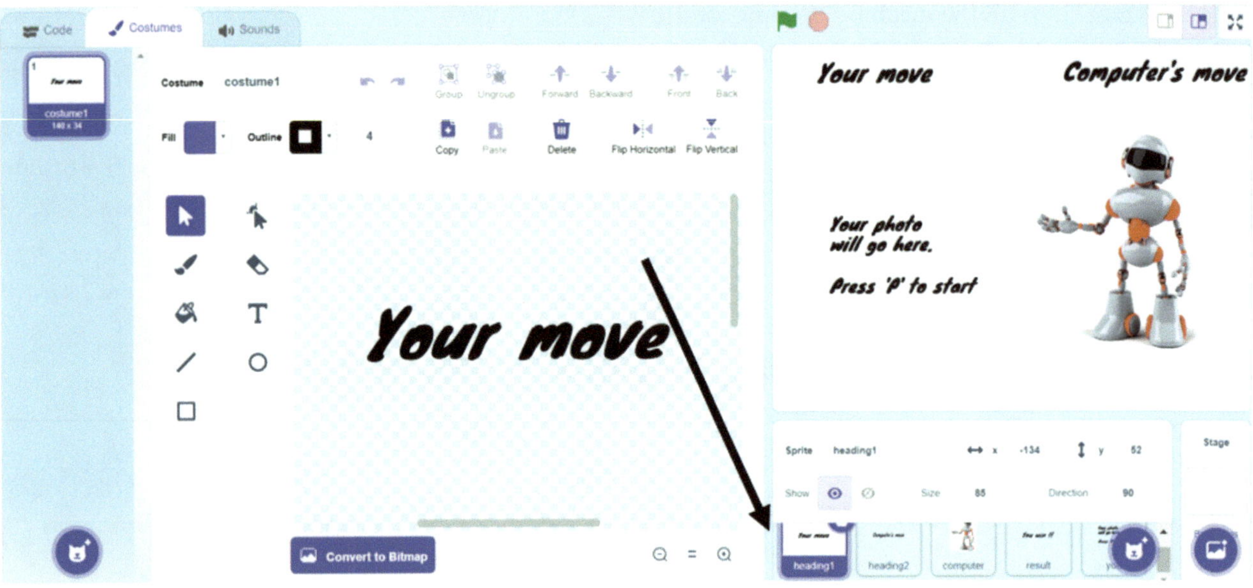

Sprite 2: heading2

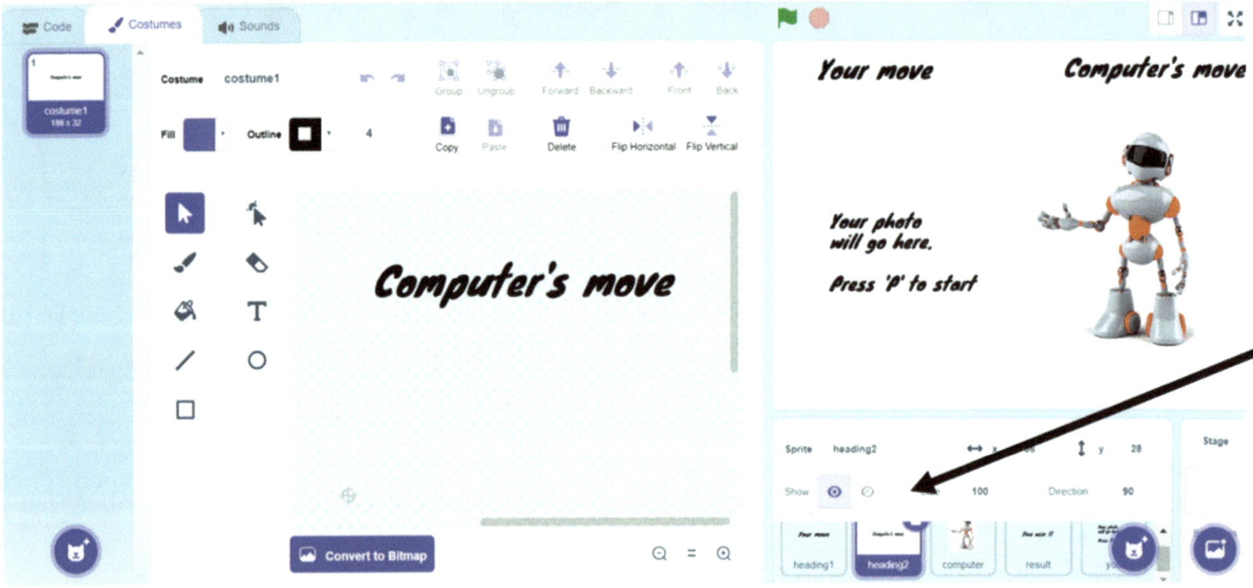

Sprite 3: computer

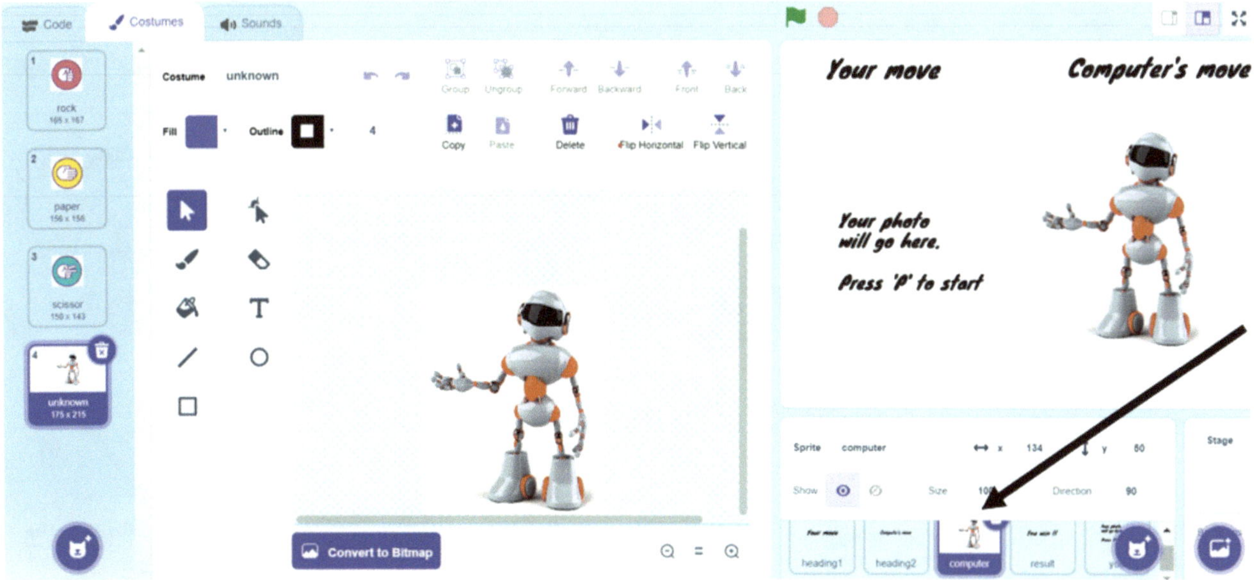

This sprite has 4 costumes: Rock, paper, scissor, unknown.
Sprite 4: result

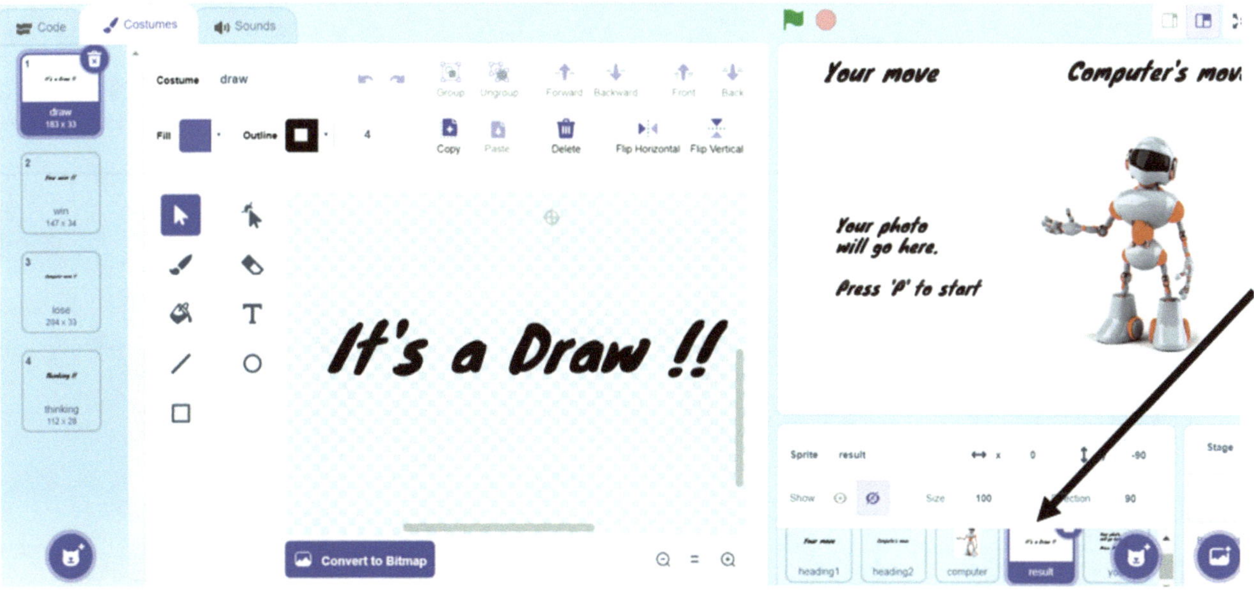

This sprite has 4 costumes: draw, win, lose, thinking.
Sprite 5: you

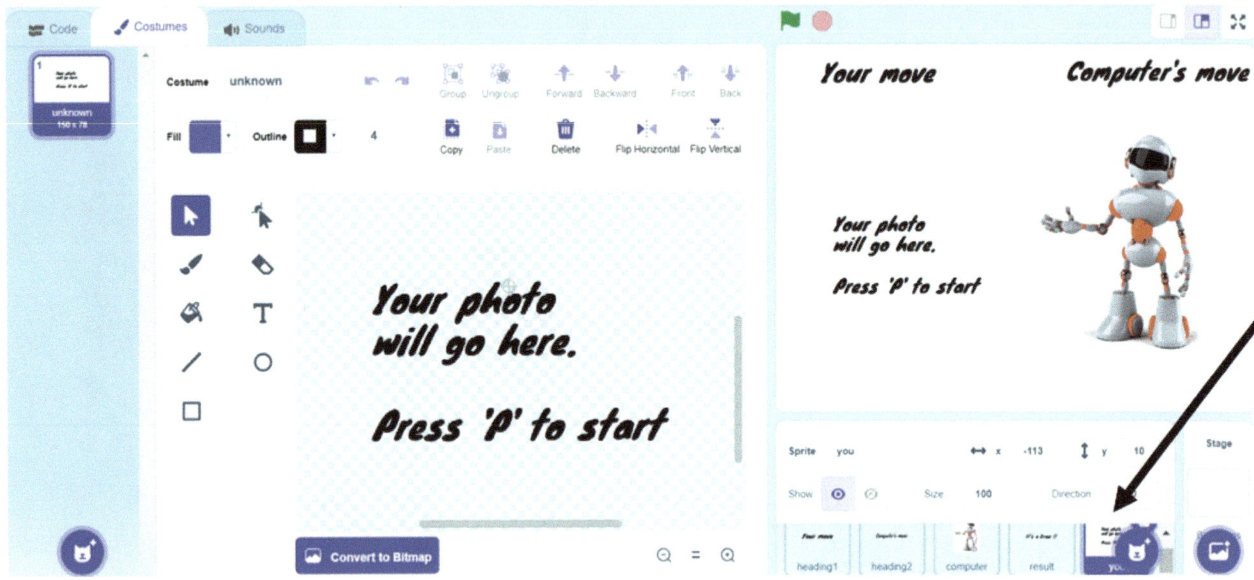

This sprite captures your webcam images.

15. Create the variables: "computer", "paper", "rock", "scissor", "you".

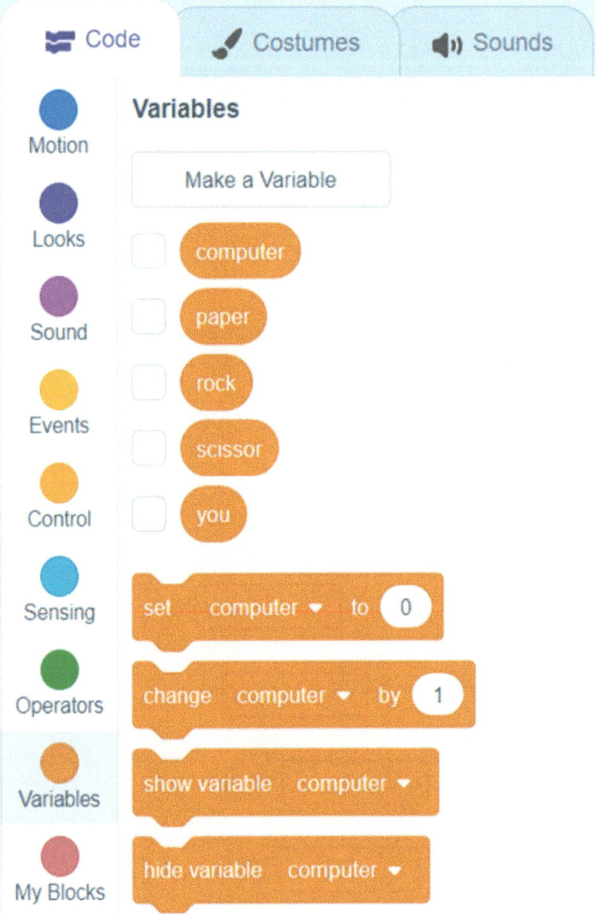

16. Click on the "Add extension" icon then click on "Video sensing".

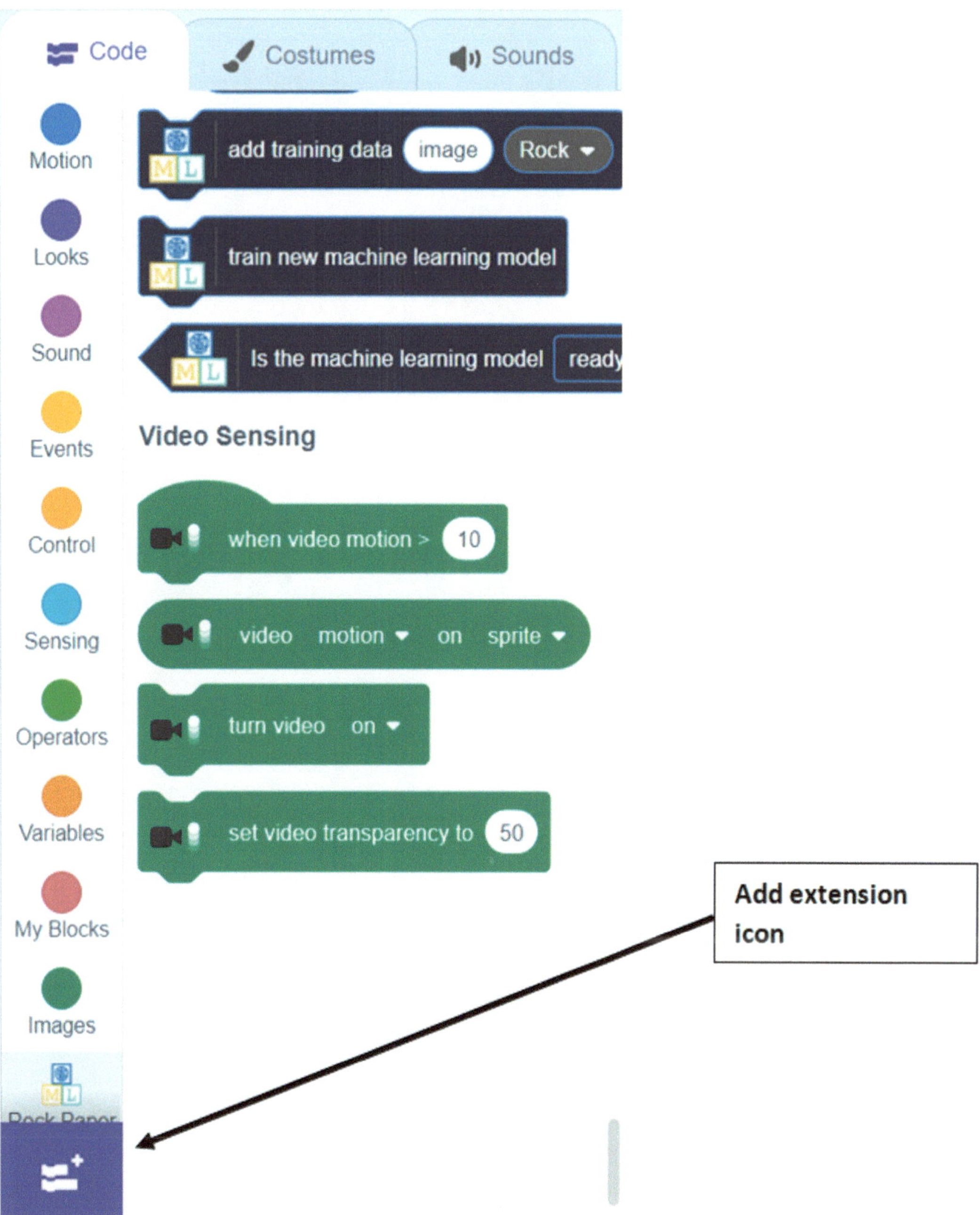

17. Adding code to the sprites.
Code for Sprite 1: heading1

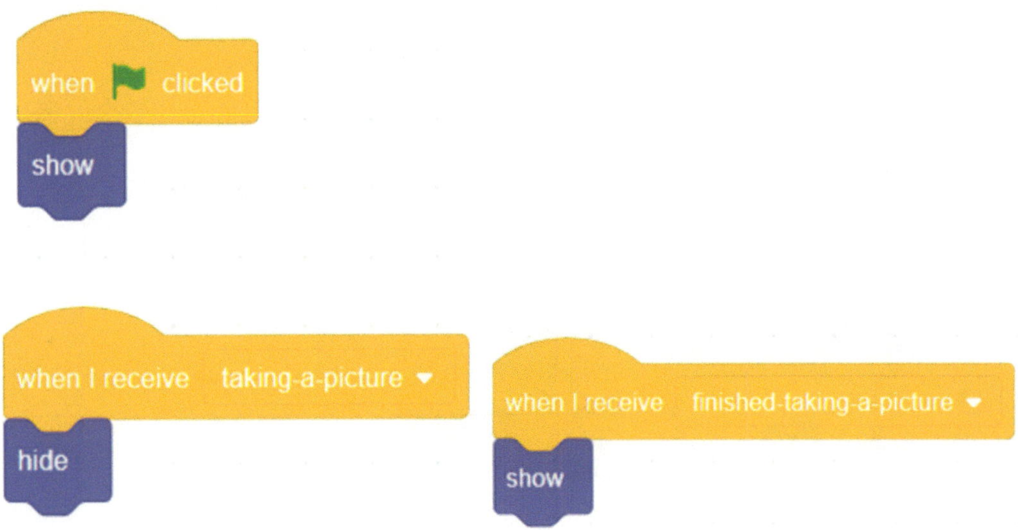

Code for Sprite 2: heading2

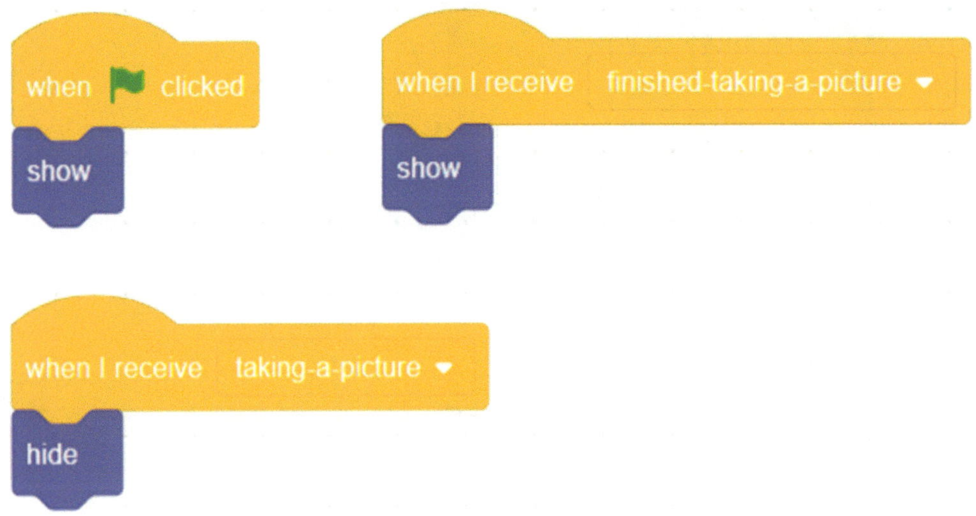

Code for Sprite 3: computer

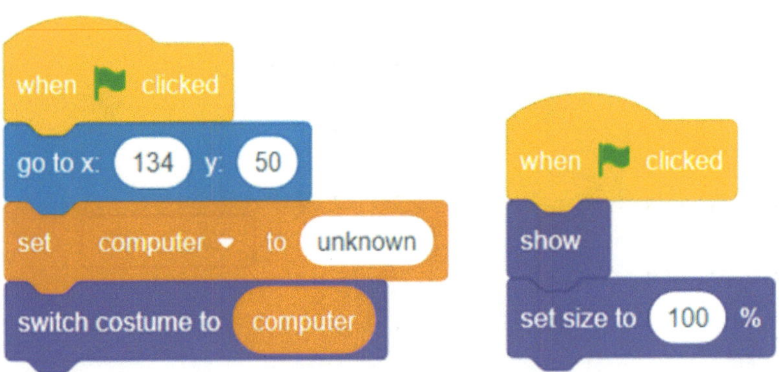

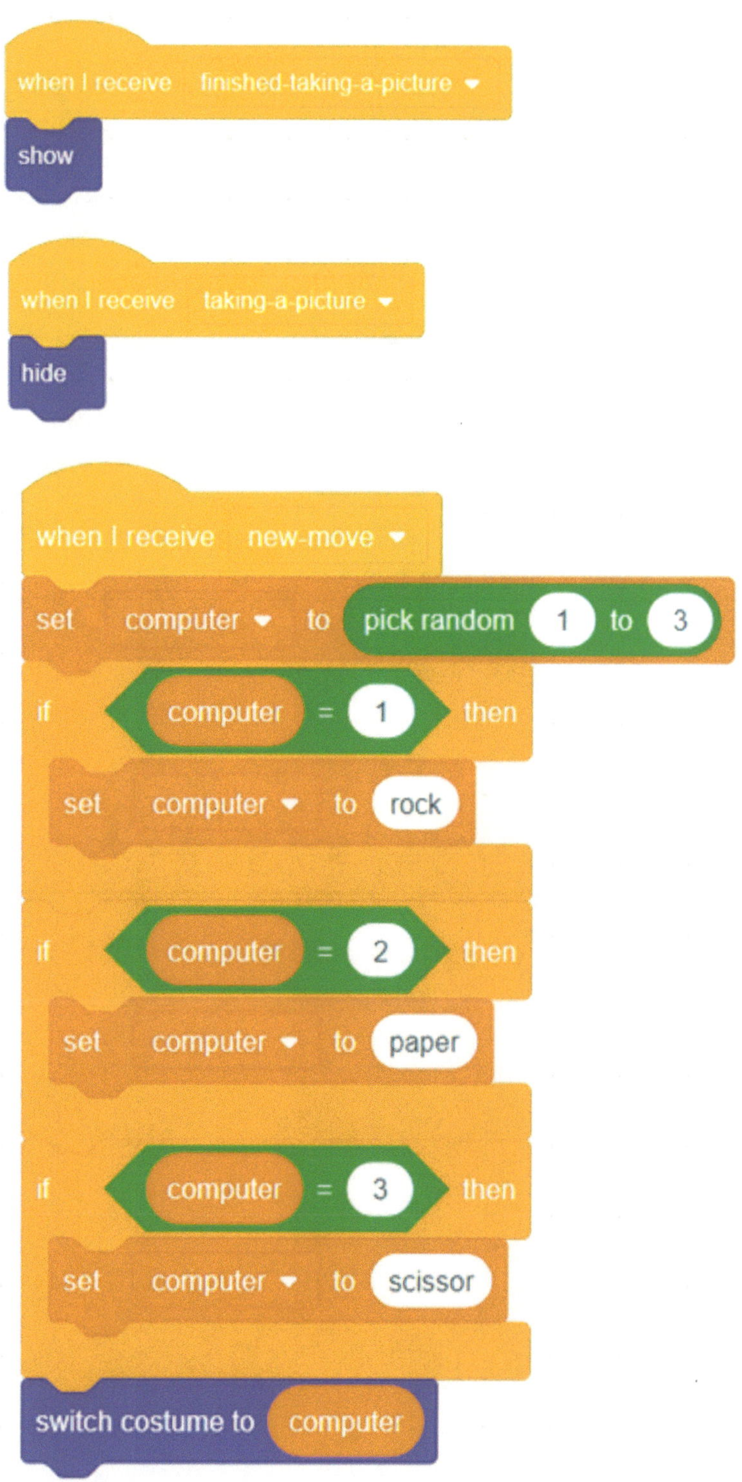

Code for Sprite 4: result

Code for Sprite 5: you

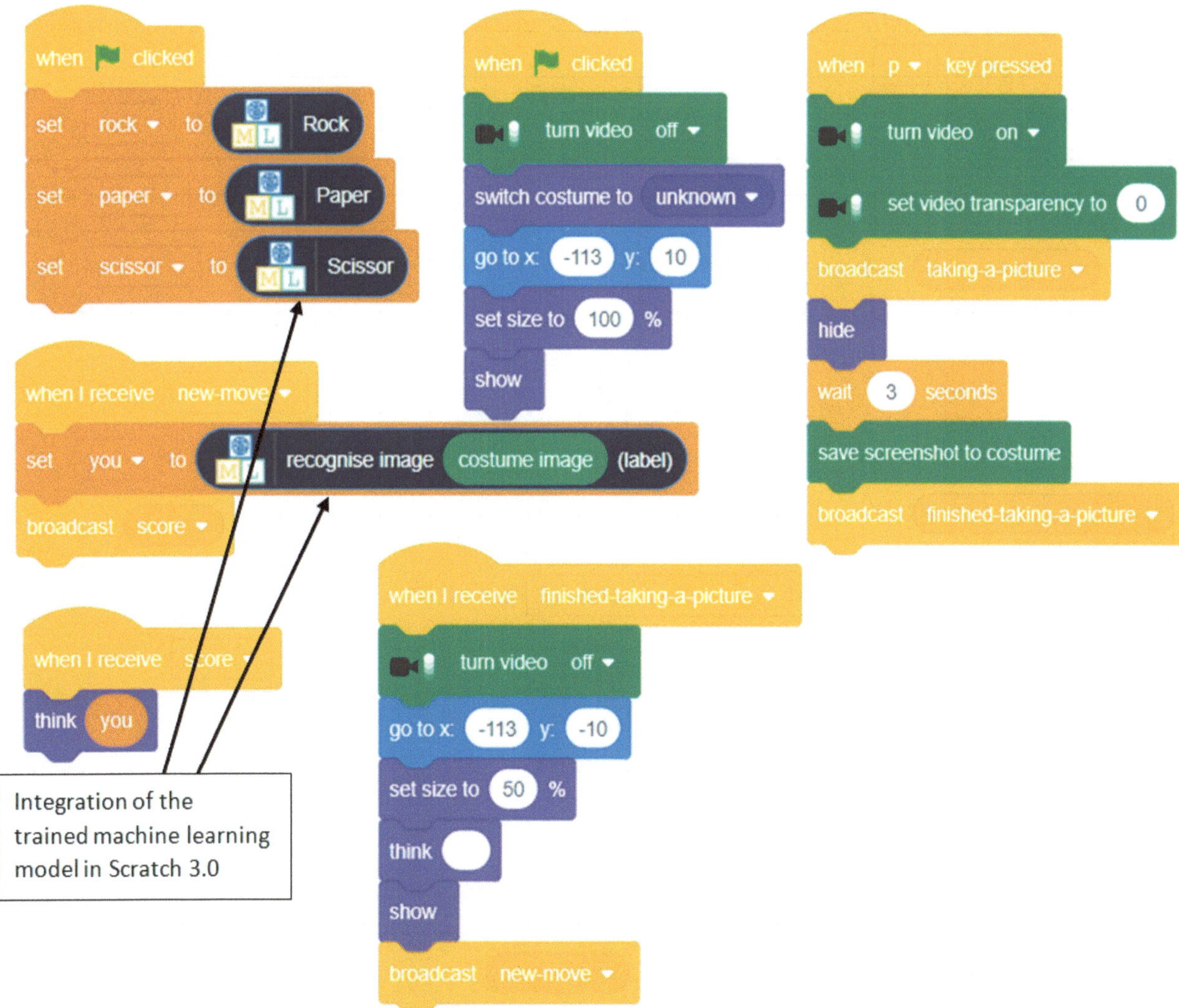

Now your program is ready. Run it by clicking on the green flag.
You will get the following outputs:

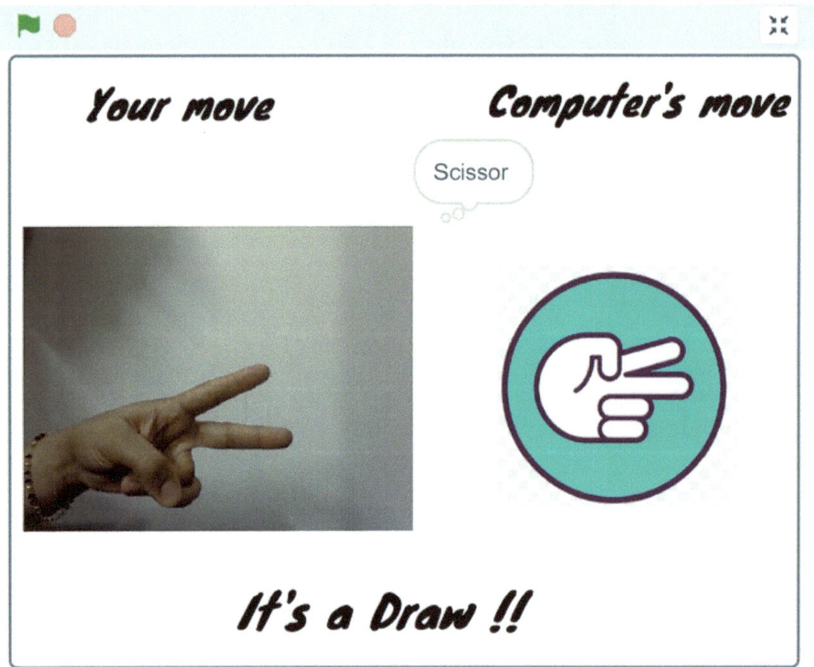

Scan the QR code to view the output of this project.

SCAN ME FOR THE OUTPUT VIDEO

SOUND RECOGNITION

CHAPTER FIVE

PROJECT 4: EMOJI RECOGNITION

OBJECTIVE: To make the computer recognize sounds and display an appropriate emoji related to that sound.
TOPICS: Sound recognition.
POINTS TO BE NOTED:

- Dragging and dropping doesn't work in Internet Explorer. You can use a different web browser instead such as Firefox or Chrome.
- You cannot drag and drop images between two different web browsers. For example, you cannot drag a picture from Chrome window to Machine Learning for kids in Firefox or vice versa.
- Only .jpg and .png images can be used otherwise an error message will be displayed.
- The more examples you give the machine learning model while training, the more efficient it will become.

STEP BY STEP EXPLAINATION OF THE PROJECT
Stage 1: Training the Machine Learning model to recognize sounds and display an appropriate emoji.

1. Click the below mentioned link and login. MACHINE LEARNING FOR KIDS: https://machinelearningforkids.co.uk/
2. Click on "Go to your Projects".

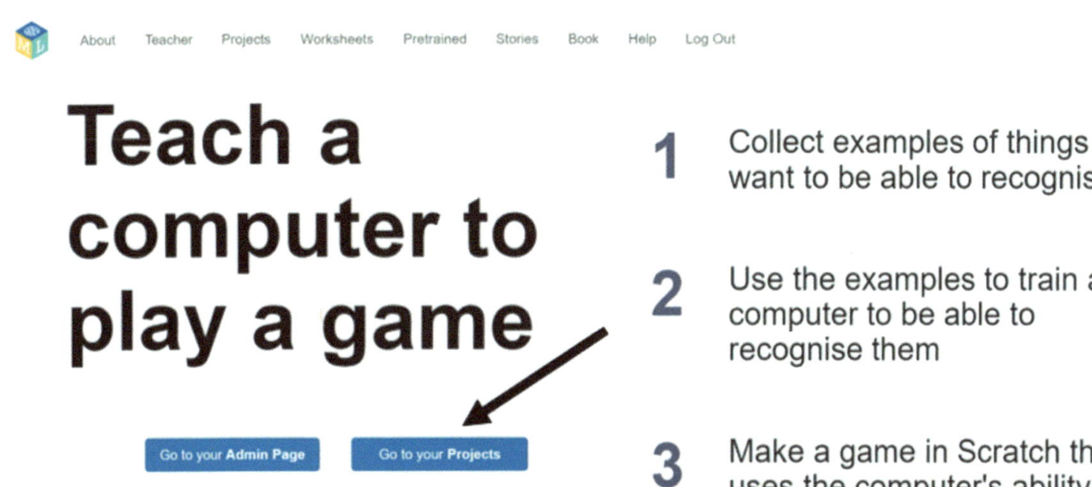

3. Click on "Add a new project".

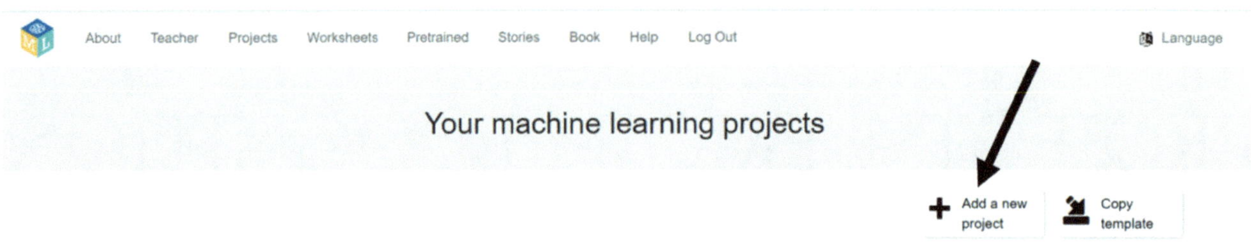

4. Enter the project name, project type and storage preference.
5. Click on "Train" to train the machine learning model.

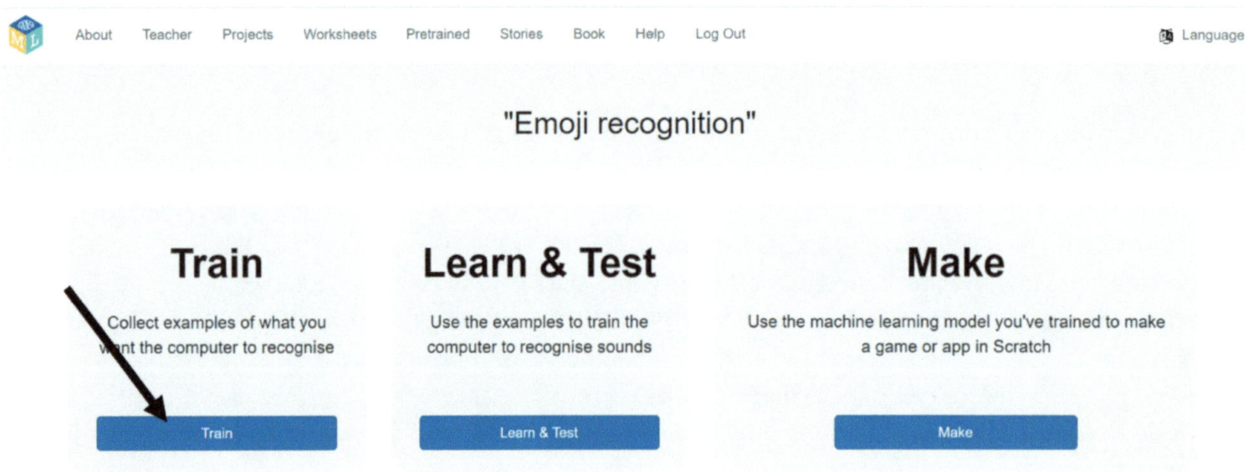

6. Click on "Add new label" and add the labels "happy", "sad", "crying", "laughing", "love". Record the background noises in the "background noise" label.

Record at least 8 examples for each label.

The more recordings you add to each label, the more efficient it becomes at recognizing sounds.

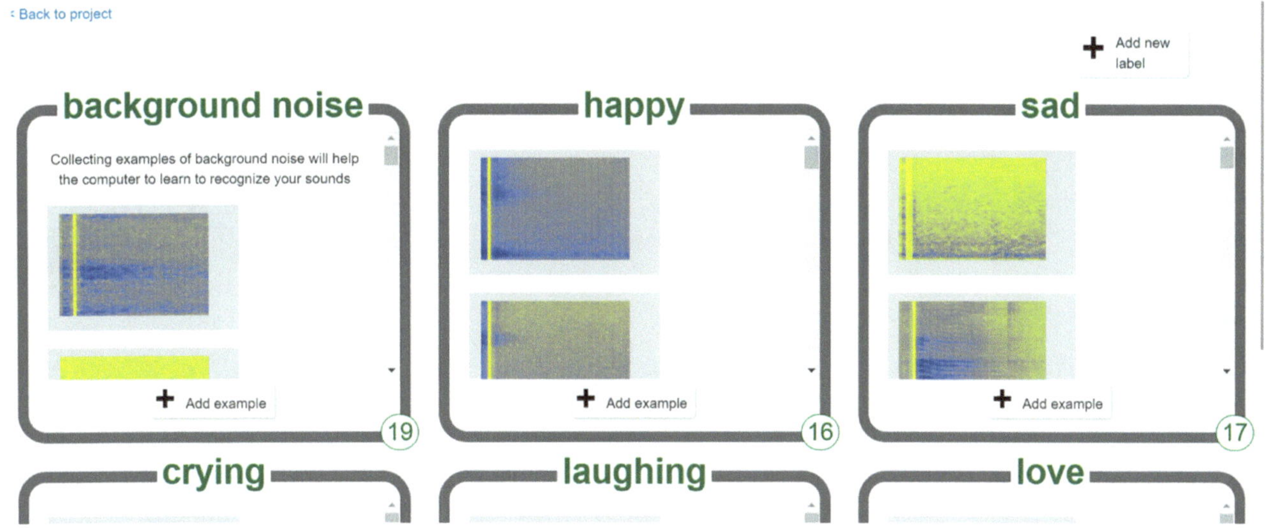

7. Click "Back to project".

8. Click on "Learn & Test".

Now record a command and check how efficient your trained machine learning model is.

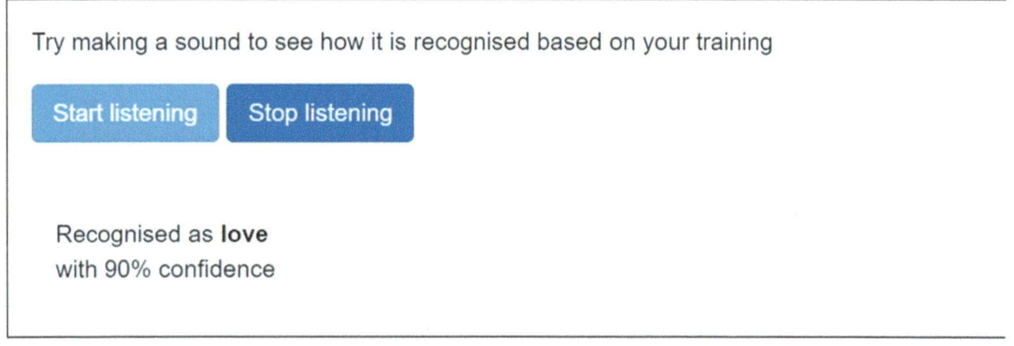

Stage 2: Coding in Scratch programming language to use the trained machine learning model.

9. Click on "Make".

Now we are going to use Scratch 3.0 to write the code to display an appropriate emoji.

Scratch 3.0 will use the machine learning model trained by us.

10. Click on "Scratch 3.0" then click on "Open in Scratch 3.0".

11. Delete the existing sprite.

12. Create a new sprite "emoji" that has 6 costumes: "happy", "sad", "crying", "laughing", "love" and "start".

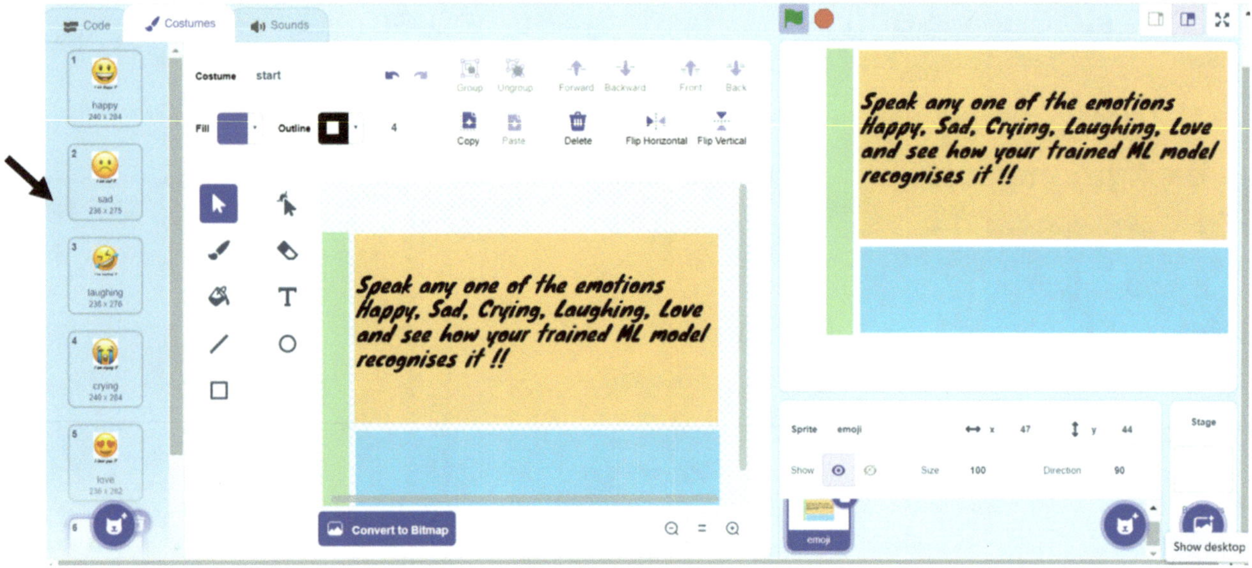

Now, copy and paste the below mentioned code in the "Code" tab.

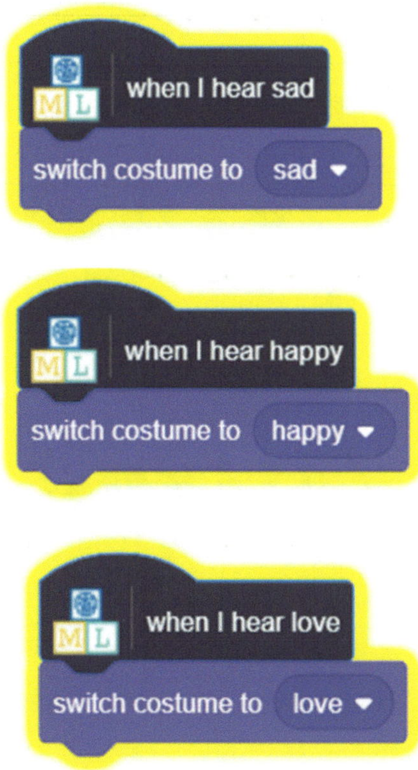

13. Click on the Green flag and run the code.
OUTPUT:

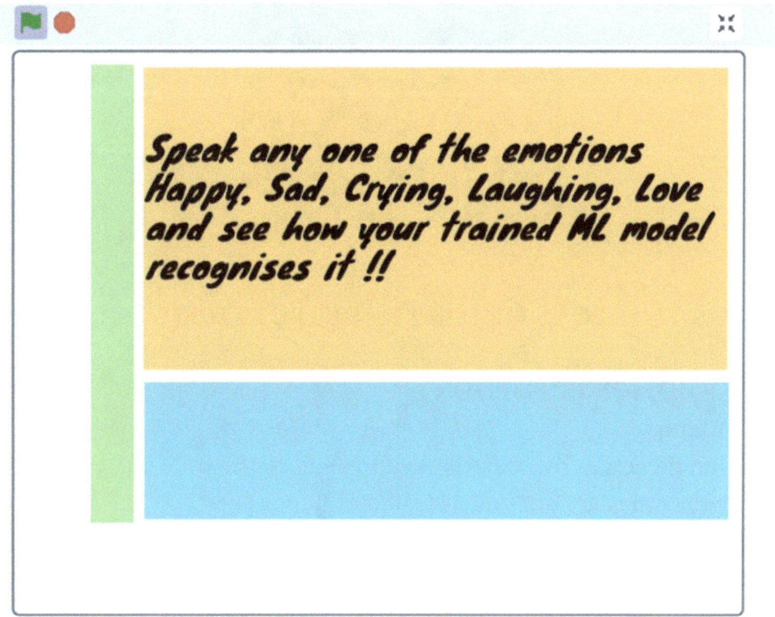

If you speak "happy", the below output will be displayed:

Scan the QR code to view the output of this project.

SCAN ME FOR THE OUTPUT VIDEO

REAL LIFE EXAMPLE OF EMOTION DETECTION
Customer Service Call Centers:
In some call centers, emotion detection software is used to analyze the tone and pitch of a caller's voice to assess their emotional state (e.g., whether they are angry, frustrated or happy).

If the software detects a stressed or upset tone, it can notify the customer service agent to handle the situation more carefully or even route the call to a manager.

This helps improve customer satisfaction by adjusting the service based on the caller's emotional needs.

This example shows sound recognition and emotion detection can be used in real-life scenarios to improve safety, convenience and customer service.

CHAPTER SIX

PROJECT 5: SMART HOMES

OBJECTIVE: To design a smart home where you can turn on and turn off the TV with your voice command.
  TOPICS: Sound recognition.
  POINTS TO BE NOTED:

- The more examples you give the machine learning model while training, the more efficient it will become.

STEP BY STEP EXPLAINATION OF THE PROJECT
Stage 1: Training the Machine Learning model to recognize sounds to turn on and turn off the TV.

1. Click the below mentioned link and login.

MACHINE LEARNING FOR KIDS: https://machinelearningforkids.co.uk/

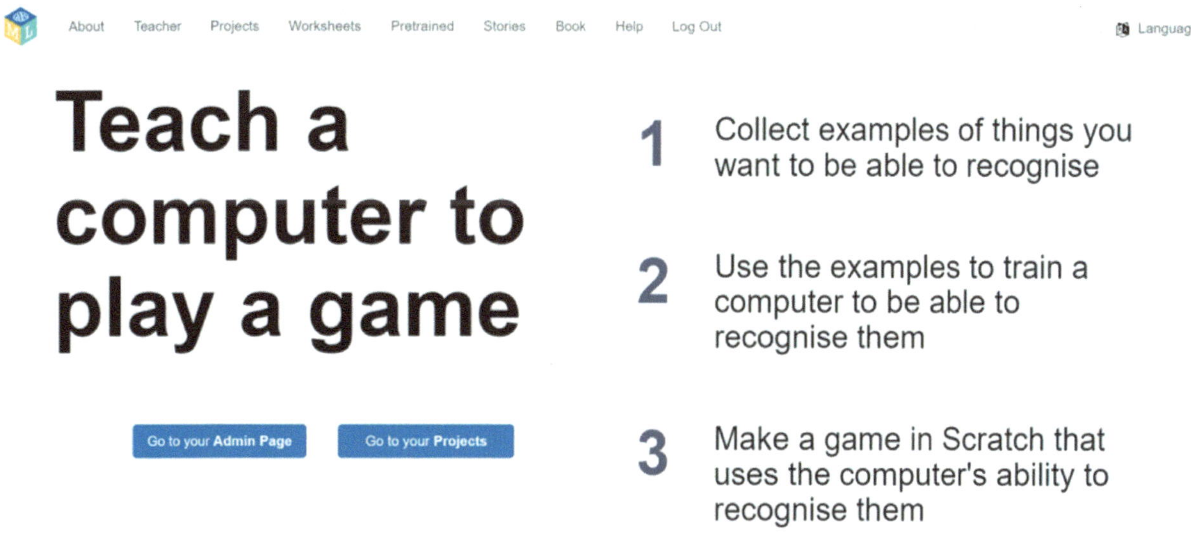

2. Click on "Go to your Projects".
3. Click on "Add a new project".
Enter the project name, project type and storage preference.

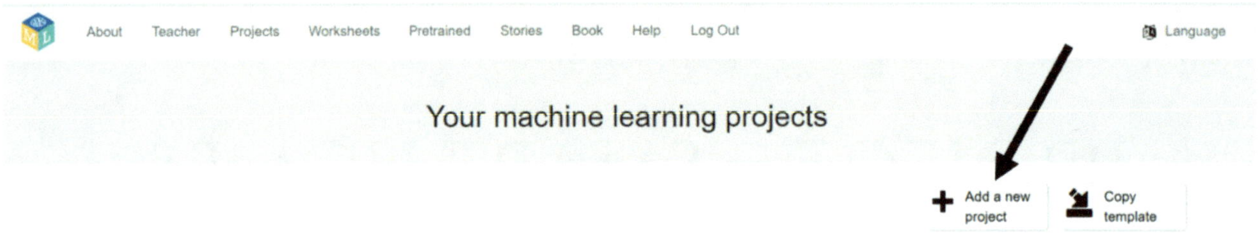

4. Click on "Train" to train the machine learning model.

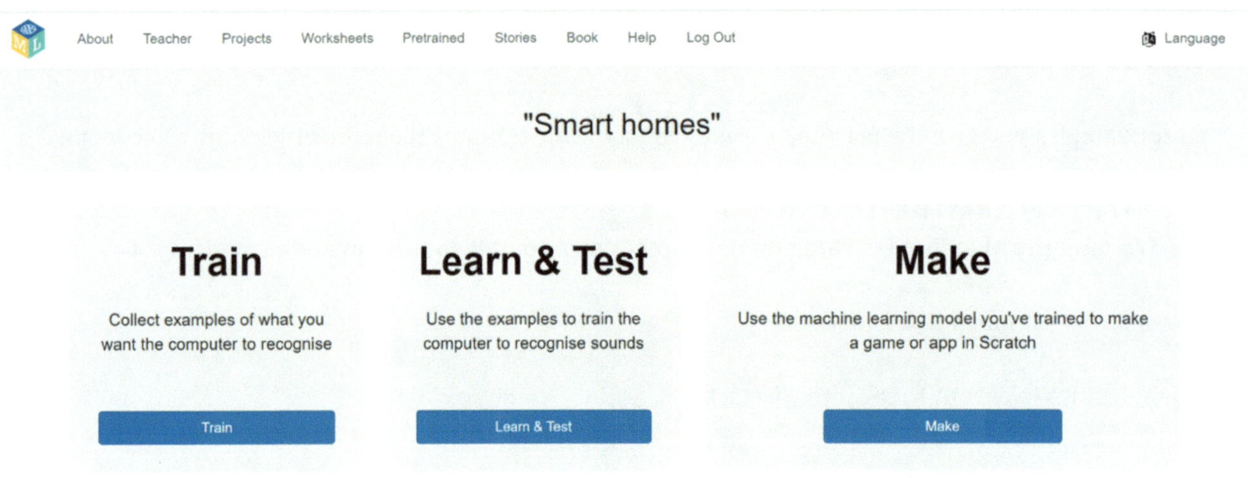

5. Click on "Add new label" and add 2 labels "tv_on" , "tv_off".
Record at least 8 examples for each label.

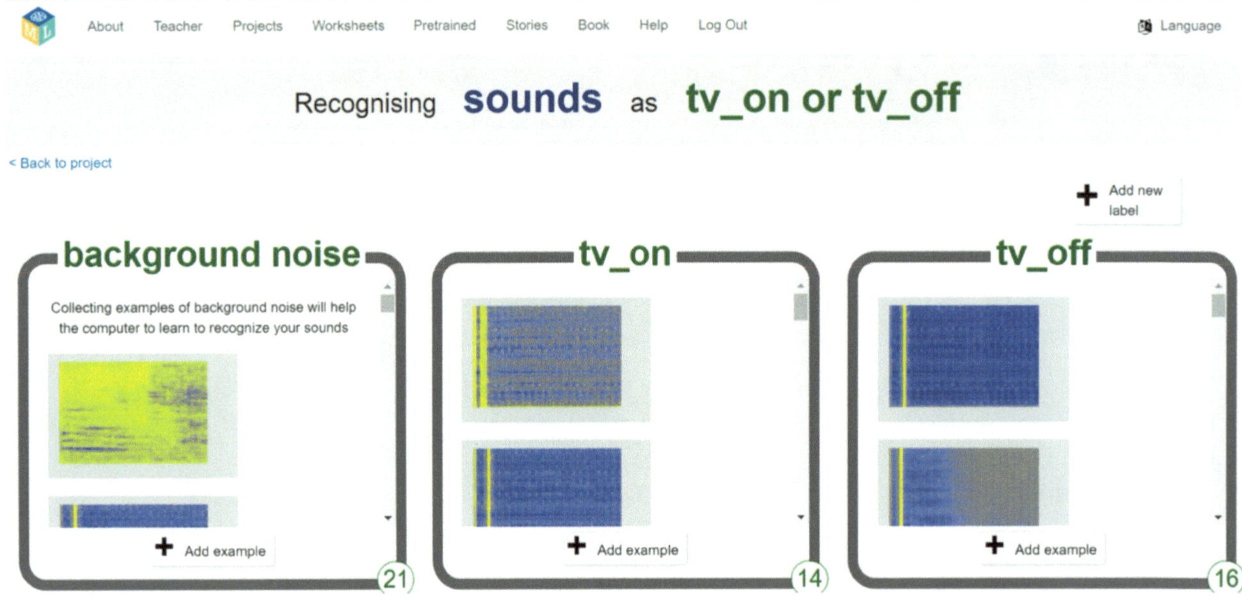

6. Click "Back to project".

7. Click on "Learn & Test".

Now record a command and check how efficient your trained machine learning model is.

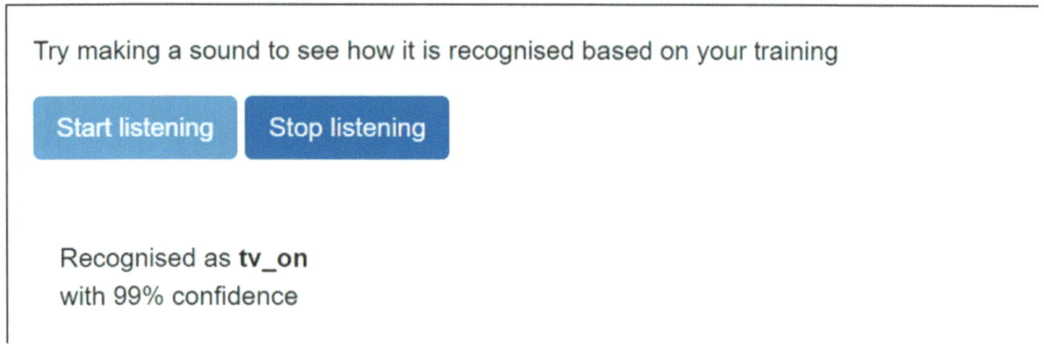

Stage 2: Coding in Scratch programming language to use the trained machine learning model.

8. Click on "Make".

Now we are going to use Scratch 3.0 to write the code to design a smart home where TV works using voice commands.

Scratch 3.0 will use the machine learning model trained by us.

9. Click on "Scratch 3.0" then click on "Open in Scratch 3.0".

10. Delete the existing sprite.

11. Create a new sprite "TV" that has 4 costumes.

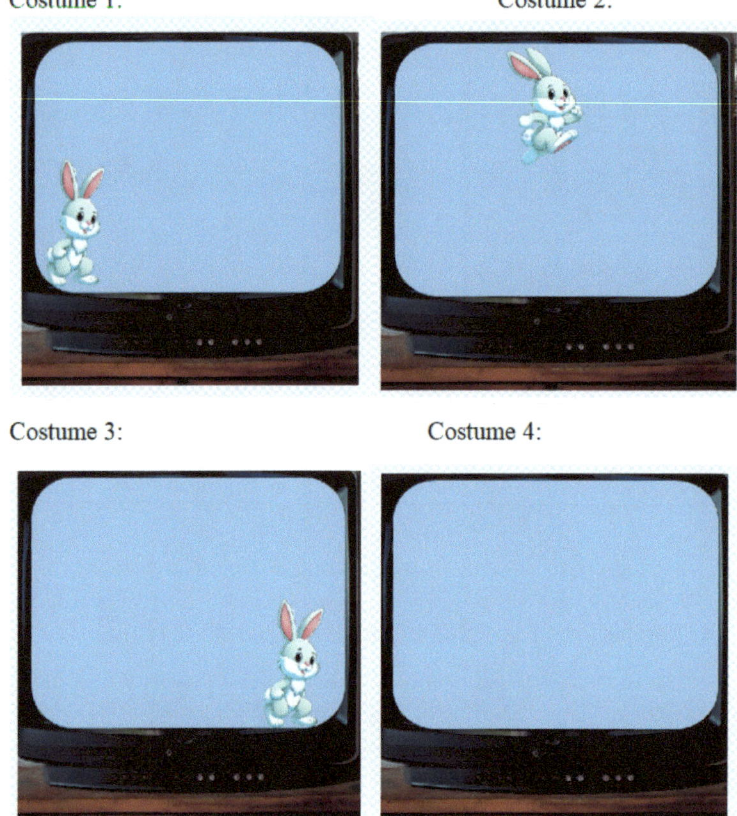

12. Create a variable "on".

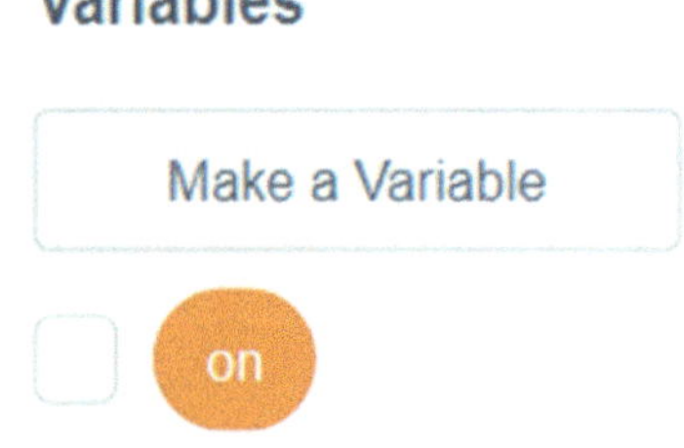

13. Now copy the below mentioned code in the "Code" tab.

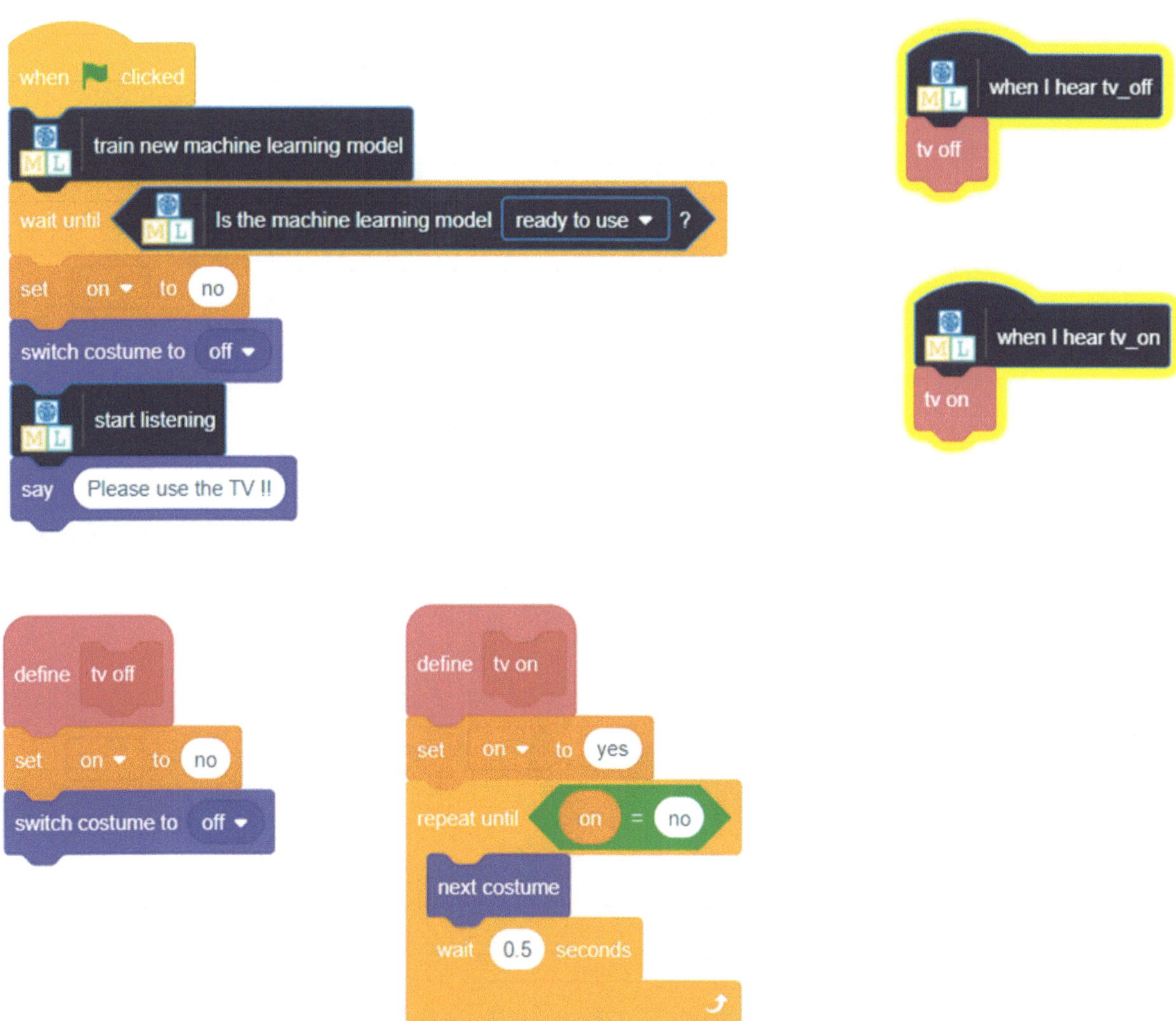

14. Click on the Green flag and run the code.
You'll see a rabbit jumping when you say "TV on" and an off TV when you say "TV off".

Scan the QR code to view the output of this project.

SCAN ME FOR THE OUTPUT VIDEO

REAL LIFE APPLICATION OF SOUND RECOGNITION IN SMART HOMES

Alexa operates smart homes using sound recognition by interpreting your voice commands and converting them into actions that control smart devices, such as lights, thermostats and security systems.

Here's how the process works in a more detailed way:

1. Wake word detection (sound recognition):

Alexa is always passively listening for a specific "wake word" like "Alexa" or "Echo". When it detects this word through sound recognition, the device activates and starts processing the audio input.

2. Speech recognition

Once Alexa hears the wake word, it listens to the rest of your command, such as "turn on the lights" or "set the thermostat to 72 degrees". This voice input is captured and converted into digital data through speech recognition. Alexa analyses the sound waves of your speech and translates them into words.

3. Natural Language Processing (NLP)

After capturing the speech, Alexa uses Natural Language Processing (NLP) to understand the meaning behind the words. It breaks down the sentence, identifies the key actions (like "turn on") and objects (like "lights" or "thermostat"), and interprets what you're asking it to do.

NUMBER RECOGNITION

CHAPTER SEVEN

PROJECT 6: JOURNEY TO THE OFFICE

Objective: To train the computer to look for patterns in how the working professionals travel to work.

Topic: Predictive machine learning model.

Pre-requisites: For this project we need to do a survey of working professionals asking their Age (in years), Travel distance (km) and their mode of transport to work (Car/Bike/Walking).The more samples we collect, more efficient the Machine learning model will become.

Sample survey data:

The below mentioned survey data is of 51 working professionals.

S.NO	MODE OF TRANSPORT TO WORK					
	CAR		BIKE		WALKING	
	Age	Distance(km)	Age	Distance(km)	Age	Distance(km)
1	28	10	35	5	42	2
2	30	15	25	3	27	1
3	40	8	31	12	46	2
4	50	20	29	4	36	4
5	28	10	35	5	24	3
6	30	15	25	3	26	2
7	40	8	31	12	33	4
8	50	20	29	4	42	3
9	33	6	26	8	45	1
10	37	18	39	7	24	3
11	48	22	32	9	46	2
12	41	11	38	12	27	1.5
13	29	5	30	10		
14	34	14	31	7		
15	52	17	35	10		
16	43	9	38	9		
17	49	15				
18	29	13				
19	40	6				
20	44	16				
21	47	8				
22	28	14				
23	50	18				

POINTS TO BE NOTED:

- The more examples you give the machine learning model while training, the more efficient it will become.

STEP BY STEP EXPLAINATION OF THE PROJECT

1. Log in to https://machinelearningforkids.co.uk/#!/login
2. Go to your projects.
3. Create a project "journey to the office".

Project type: recognizing numbers. Add Values "Age (yrs)" and "Distance (km)".

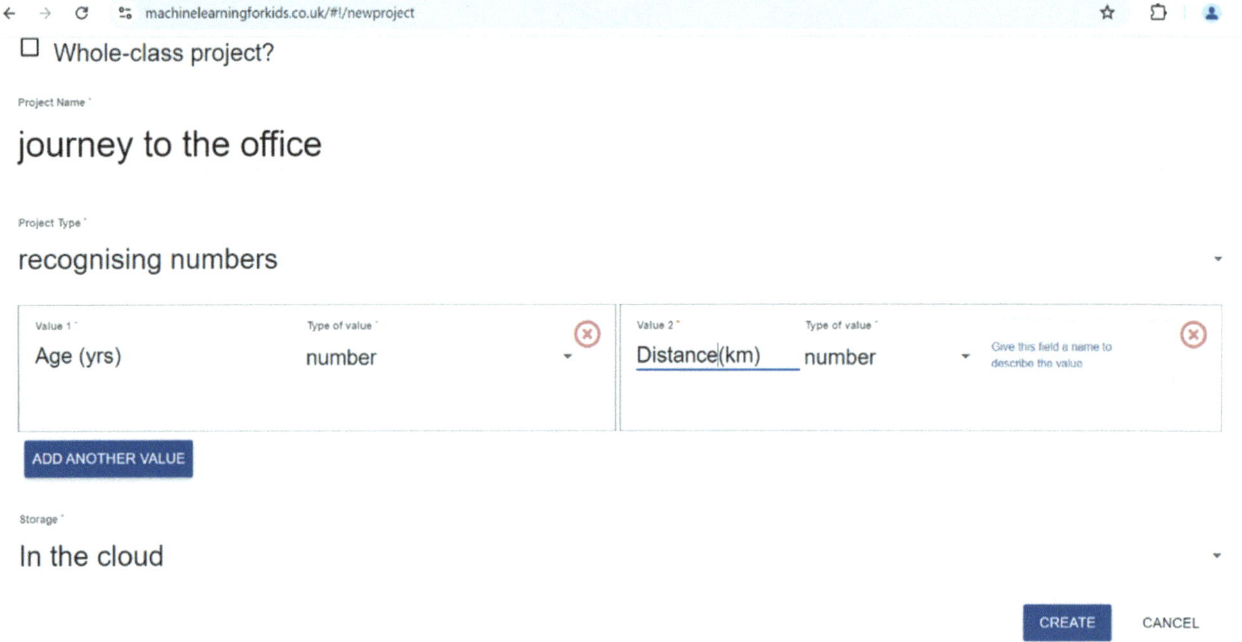

4. Add labels "Car", "Bike" and "Walking". Add examples in the respective labels from the above survey data.

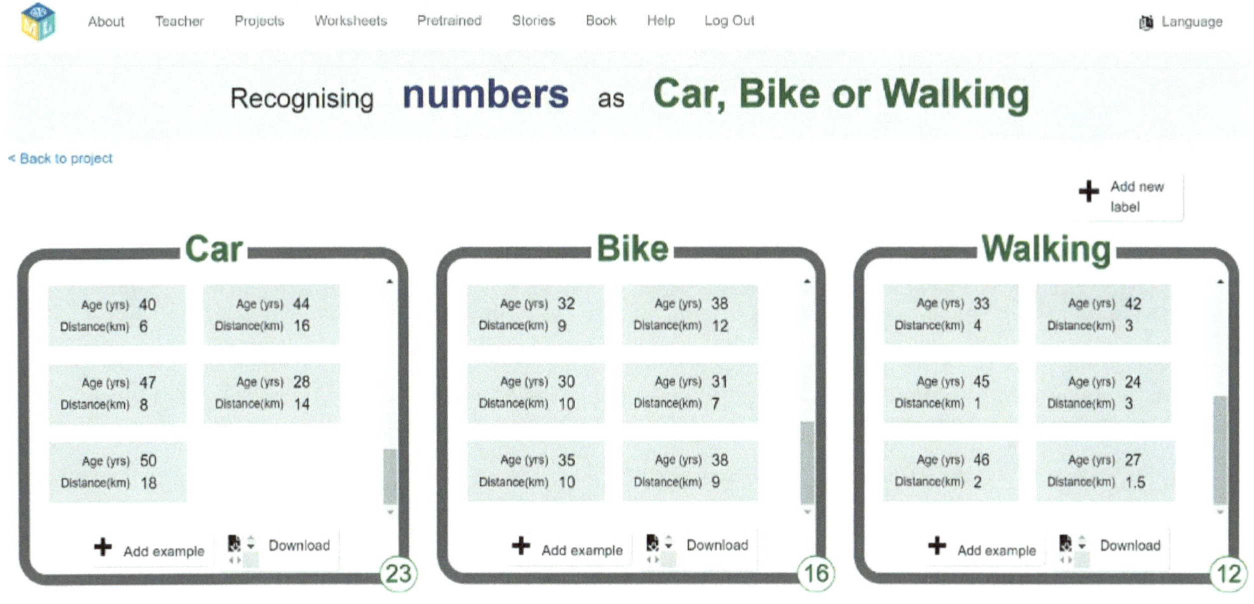

5. Click on "Back to project". Click on "Learn & Test".
Now, test you trained Machine Learning model.

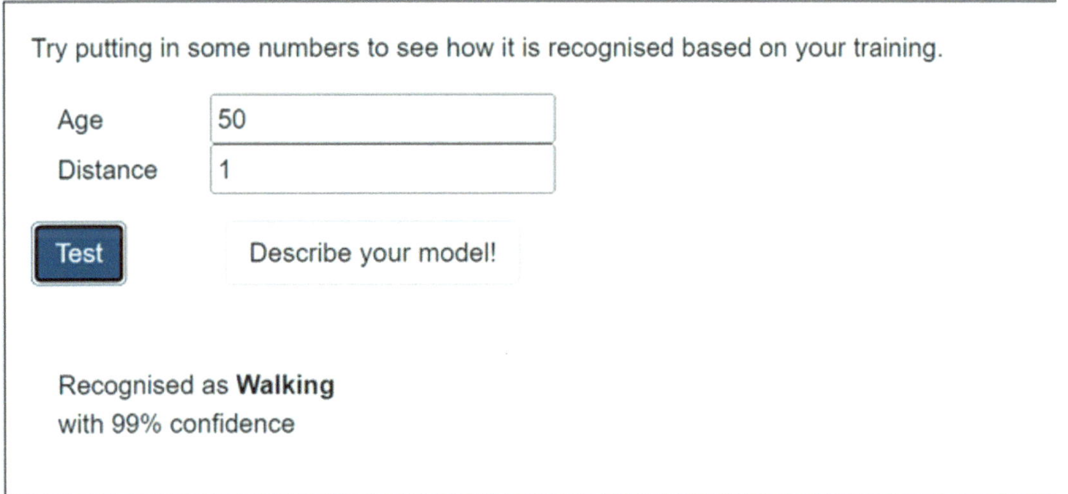

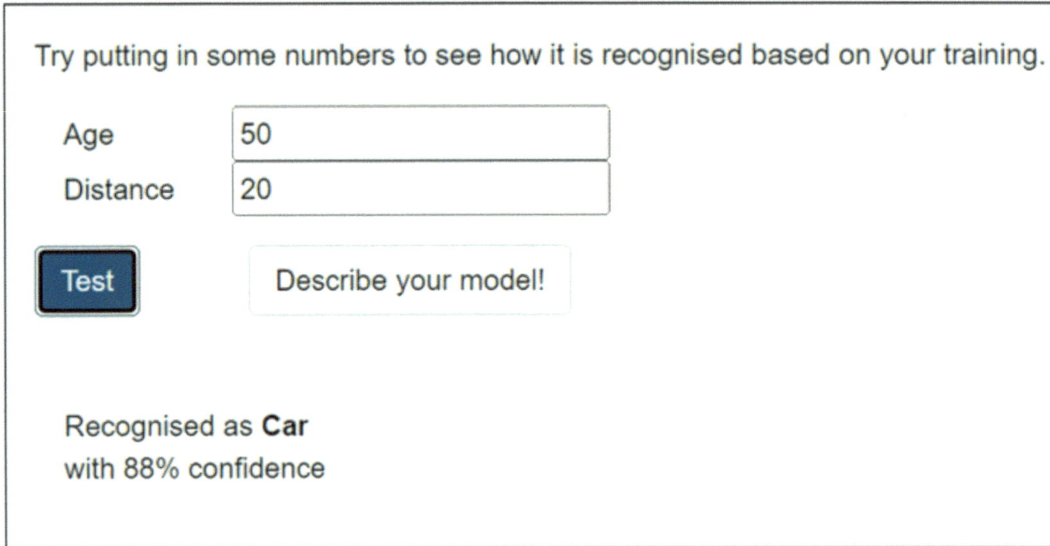

You will notice that the computer understands when Age increases and the distance is more, the professional will prefer a car rather than walking to work.

In Scratch programming language we need to create 1 sprite, 2 variables and 1 block.

This is how the screen will look.

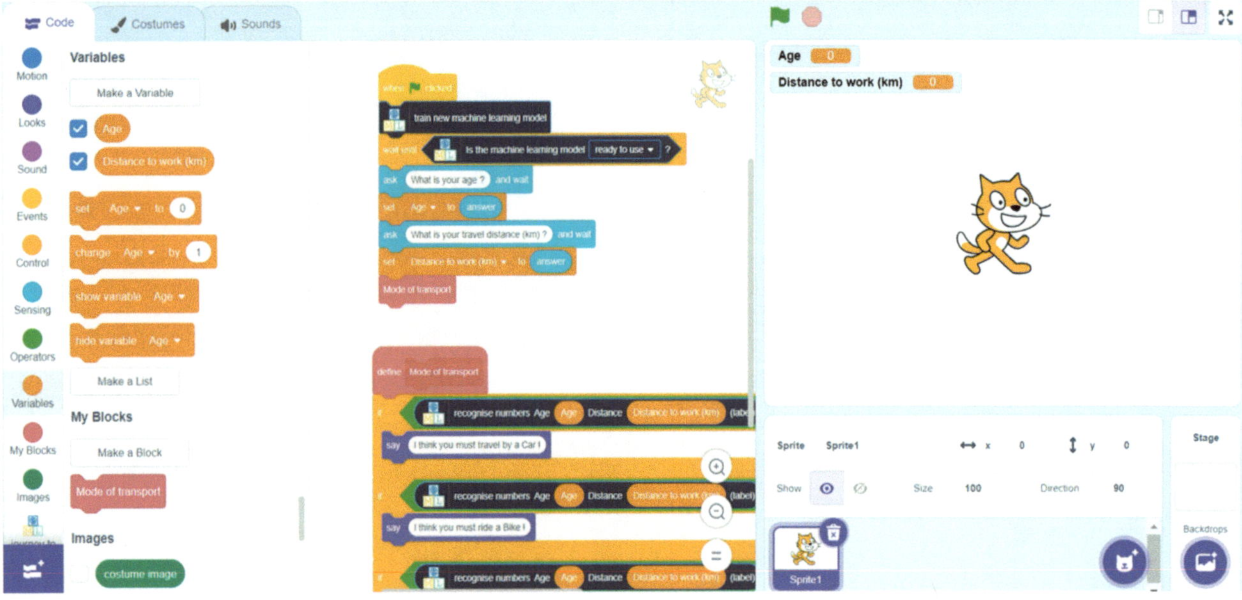

6. Create 2 variables "Age" and "Distance to work (km)".

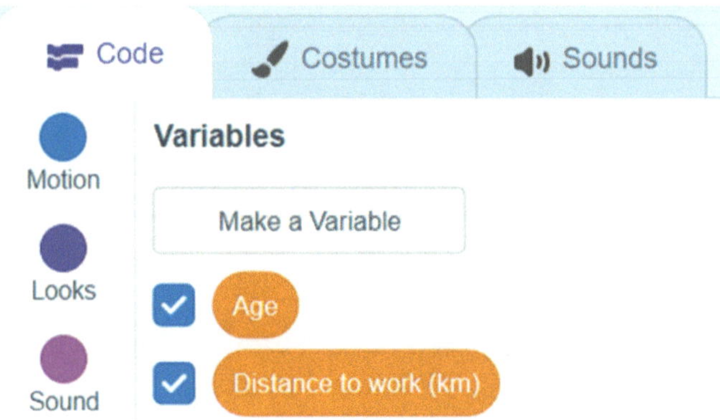

7. Create a block "Mode of transport" that predicts what will be the appropriate mode of transport for the specified age and travel distance.

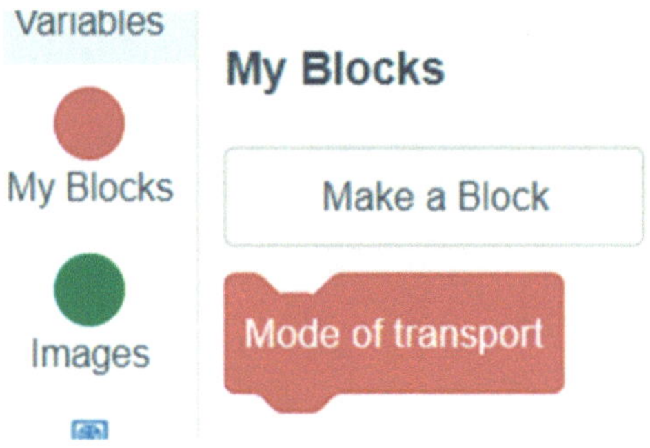

8. Copy the below mentioned code.

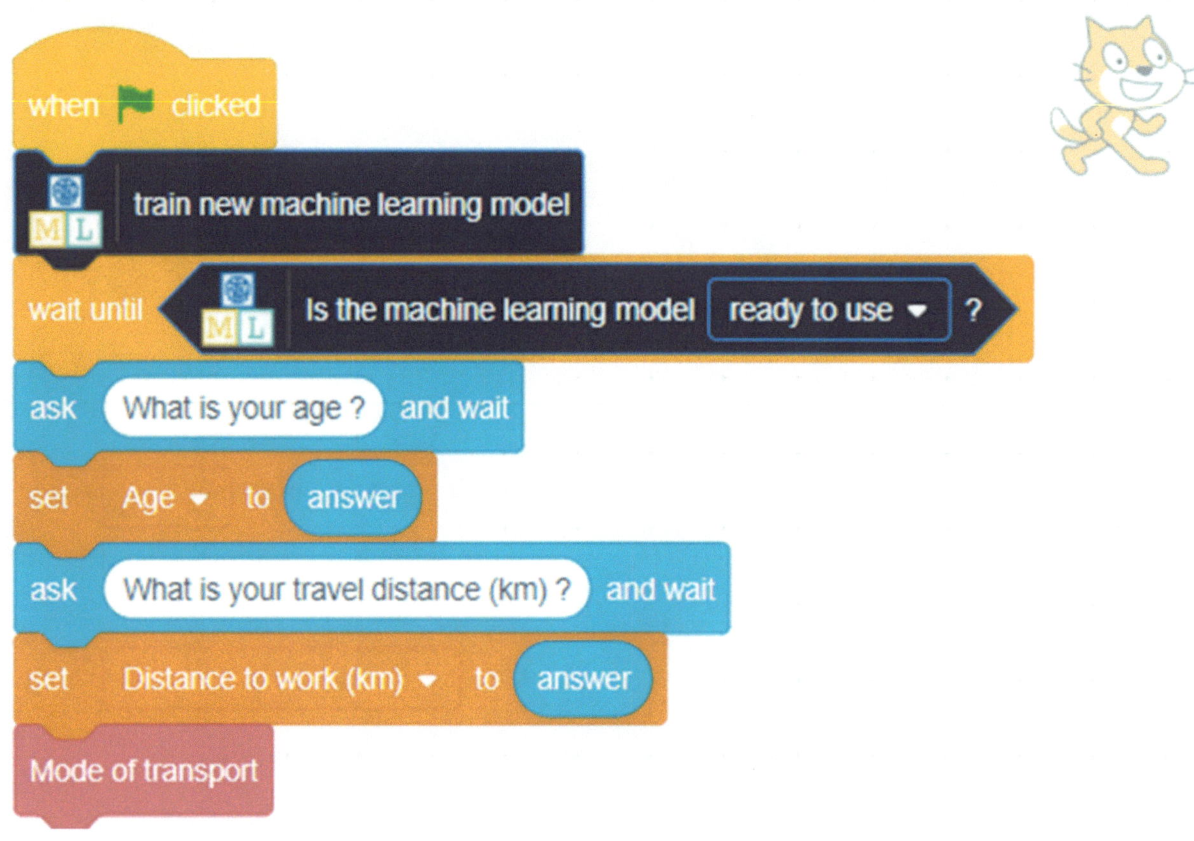

when [flag] clicked
train new machine learning model
wait until Is the machine learning model [ready to use ▼] ?
ask [What is your age ?] and wait
set [Age ▼] to (answer)
ask [What is your travel distance (km) ?] and wait
set [Distance to work (km) ▼] to (answer)
Mode of transport

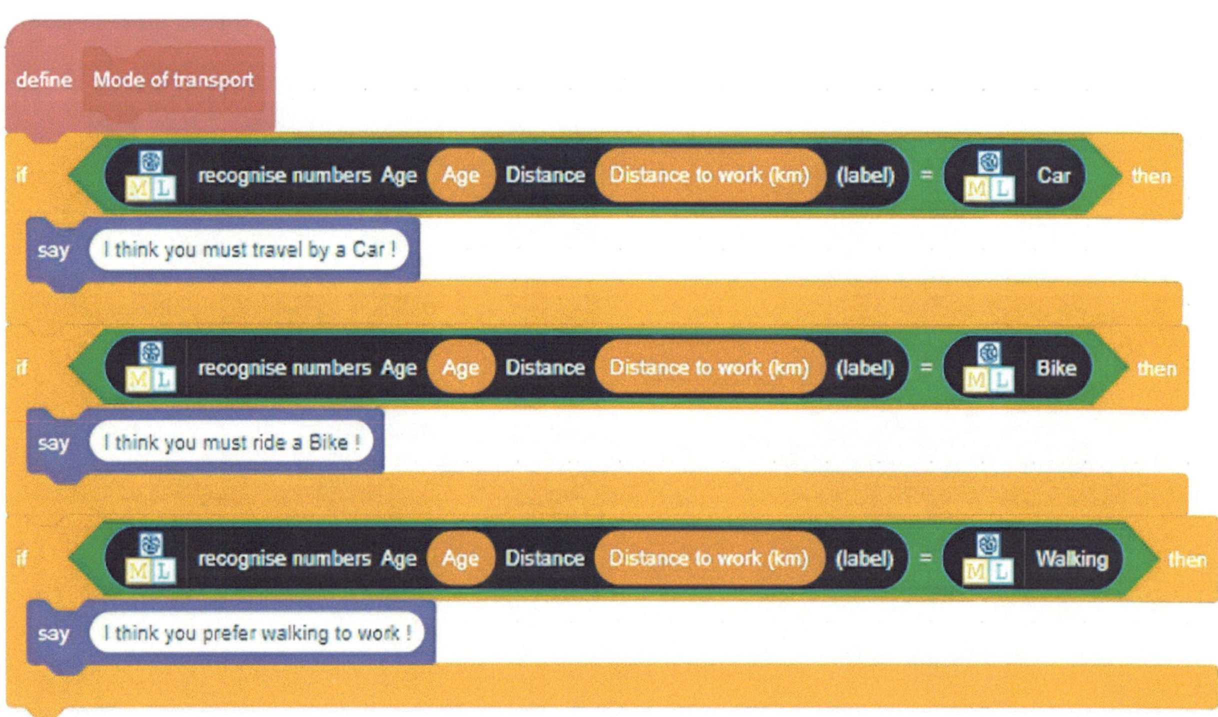

define Mode of transport
if < recognise numbers Age (Age) Distance (Distance to work (km)) (label) = Car > then
say [I think you must travel by a Car !]
if < recognise numbers Age (Age) Distance (Distance to work (km)) (label) = Bike > then
say [I think you must ride a Bike !]
if < recognise numbers Age (Age) Distance (Distance to work (km)) (label) = Walking > then
say [I think you prefer walking to work !]

Now, click the full screen button and then the Green flag.

In this project we have trained the computer to understand how a person's mode of transport is dependent on his age and the distance to be travelled.

OUTPUT:

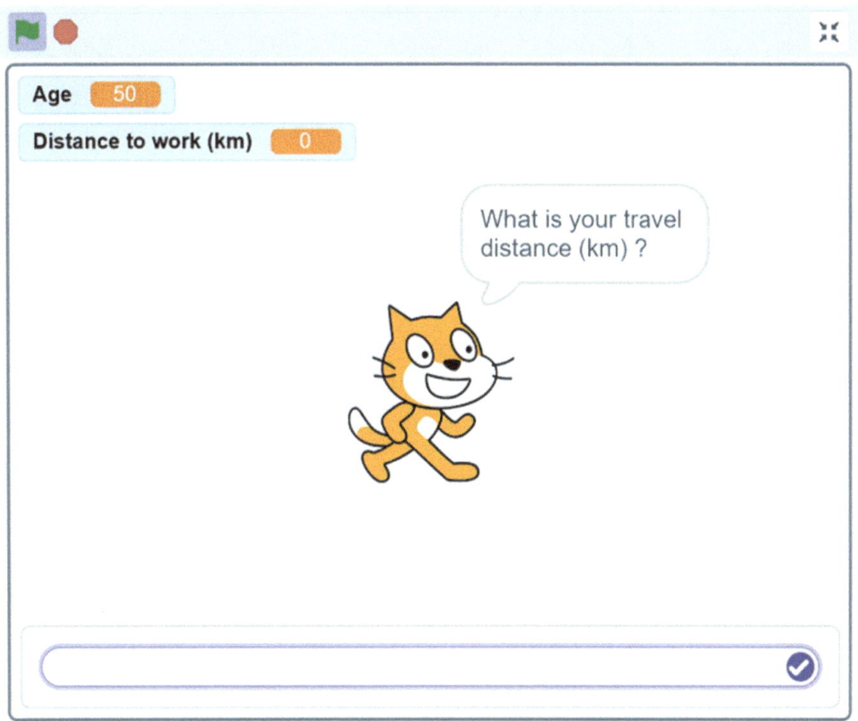

Scan the QR code to view the output of this project.

SCAN ME FOR THE OUTPUT VIDEO

REAL-LIFE APPLICATIONS OF PREDICTIVE MACHINE LEARNING MODEL THAT USES NUMBER RECOGNITION

- **Navigation apps like Google Maps:**

These apps use machine learning models to predict the shortest travel time between two locations. The model analyzes historical traffic data, real-time traffic conditions, road closures, and various other factors to estimate how long it will take to travel. Based on this prediction, the app suggests the fastest route for drivers, often recalculating if conditions change, such as sudden traffic jams or accidents.

- **Automatic cheque deposit systems in bank**

When a customer deposits a cheque through an ATM or a mobile banking app, the system uses machine learning models to recognize and predict the handwritten or printed numbers on the cheque such as the account number, cheque amount and routing numbers. The machine learning model has been trained on thousands of samples of handwritten digits to accurately interpret and predict the numbers, even with variations in handwriting styles. This makes the cheque deposit process faster and reduces errors compared to manual entry.

Glossary

Artificial Intelligence (AI): A field of computer science that enables machines to simulate human intelligence.

Machine Learning (ML): A branch of AI where machines learn from data to make decisions or predictions.

Training Data: Information used to teach a machine learning model.

Model: A computer program trained to recognize patterns and make decisions.

Scratch 3.0: A visual programming language designed for children to create interactive stories, games, and animations.

Image Recognition: The ability of a machine to identify and classify objects within images.

Sound Recognition: The ability of a machine to interpret and respond to different audio inputs.

Number Recognition: Teaching a machine to identify handwritten or typed numbers.

ML for Kids: A platform that helps children build machine learning projects in a simple and visual way.

www.ingramcontent.com/pod-product-compliance
Lightning Source LLC
Chambersburg PA
CBHW041642110726
48005CB00003B/687